CONNECT & SUCCEED

A Communication Style to
Engage and Motivate Your Employees

CONNECT & SUCCEED

A Communication Style to
Engage and Motivate Your Employees

David W. Bennett, Ph.D.

GeniusWork Publishing
Los Angeles, CA

Published by GeniusWork Publishing
www.geniusworkpublishing.com

Printed in the United States of America
Cover Design by Sakada

Library of Congress Control Number: 2015958598

Cataloging-in-Publication data is on file with the publisher.

ISBN   978-0-9831393-4-8 (paperback)
ISBN   978-0-9831393-5-5 (ebk)
ISBN   978-0-9831393-6-2 (ebk)

To Sakada,
whose coaching and counsel
made this book possible.

TABLE OF CONTENTS

I. SUCCESS

CHAPTER 1: Engage and Motivate   3

CHAPTER 2: The Connect & Succeed Style   19

II. ENERGETIC LISTENING

CHAPTER 3: Pay Attention   35

CHAPTER 4: Pinpoint the Nonverbals   55

III. TARGETED SPEAKING

CHAPTER 5: Speak With Clarity   73

CHAPTER 6: Support the Speaker   97

IV. COMMON GROUND CONNECTION

CHAPTER 7: Connect Through Common Ground   121

CHAPTER 8: Your Connect & Succeed Strategy   141

AFTERWORD: Connect & Succeed   153

Works Cited   155

Index   157

About the Author   161

LIST OF EXERCISES

EXERCISE 1: Distraction Prevention   39

EXERCISE 2: Create A Trigger   41

EXERCISE 3: Power Hours   42

EXERCISE 4: Meditation   43

EXERCISE 5: Attention Span Techniques   43

EXERCISE 6: Your Self-Awareness   45

EXERCISE 7: Tone And Language   48

EXERCISE 8: What is Not Being Said   49

EXERCISE 9: Develop a Stronger Sensitivity   51

EXERCISE 10: Emotional Contagion   52

EXERCISE 11: Identify & Translate Nonverbal Signals   63

EXERCISE 12: Clustering Nonverbals   65

EXERCISE 13: Nonverbal Baselines   66

EXERCISE 14: Pinpointing The Nonverbals   68

EXERCISE 15: Match Vocabularies   77

EXERCISE 16: Do Not Offend   79

EXERCISE 17: Short Increments   81

EXERCISE 18: Match Your Verbal & Nonverbal Signals   84

EXERCISE 19: Match Nonverbal Signals   85

EXERCISE 20: Tune Into Your Emotions   87

EXERCISE 21: Use Emotional Contagion   88

EXERCISE 22: Mutual Understanding   92

EXERCISE 23: Identify And Speak Of Common Ground   94

EXERCISE 24: Audio Flow Comments   100

EXERCISE 25: Paraphrasing   100

EXERCISE 26: Questions & Comments   102

EXERCISE 27: Nonverbal Acknowledgments   107

EXERCISE 28: Spotlight The Common Ground   112

EXERCISE 29: Deal With Disagreement   115

EXERCISE 30: Mindset   126

EXERCISE 31: Connect Through Common Ground   129

EXERCISE 32: Thought Speed Gap   133

EXERCISE 33: Thin Slice Perceptions   138

EXERCISE 34: Create A Fully Formed Perspective   139

EXERCISE: 35: Are You Ready To Connect & Succeed?   146

EXERCISE 36: Goals And Timeline   148

I.
SUCCESS

CHAPTER ONE

Engage and Motivate

Communication is the critical thread that runs through everything you do as a manager, and is therefore the key factor in your success. It is estimated that between 50-70% of a manager's time is spent communicating with employees. Therefore, creating a powerful and effective communication style is important to any manager who wants to be successful.

Your communication style is important because as a manager you are the bridge between the executive level and your employees. This is a pivotal role because employees expect to be kept in the loop and will look for most of their information to come from their immediate manager. This is you.

Your communication style is also important because as the manager you set the tone for your employee's worklife. A Dale Carnegie study reports that "84% of how employees feel about their organization is driven by their immediate manager" (Dale Carnegie Training).

So the way in which you communicate your department's goals and objectives is critical to how engaged and motivated your employees feel about these goals and objectives. The way you communicate sets the tone when dealing with employee development or problems. Your ability to build strong relationships with your employees sets your department up for success. These relationships are built on communication.

Finally, your communication style will determine the overall success of your department, and the company as a whole. As a manager you must oversee projects for your company. This often means you will be directing a diverse group of employees with a variety of personalities, approaches to work, and skill levels. With good communication, these projects will get done, get done well, and your department's overall productivity will shine.

The extra-credit gold star to all of this is that the better your communication style, the bigger your own career success.

CONNECTION-LEVEL COMMUNICATION

Yes, communication is extremely important to your success as a manager, but communication itself can be the simple relaying of information to your employees. As a manager this might mean you communicate the instructions, deadlines, and information about a project to the employees who are going to complete the project for you. How the information is received by the employees is not a factor in the basic definition of this communication.

If though, as a manager, you want to not just communicate the information, but you also want to engage and motivate your employees to the successful completion of the project, you will want to not just communicate, but also connect with those employees. This is where your communication style can make all the difference. You want a style that allows you to connect and succeed.

The Connect and Succeed definition of connection is to use your conversations with an employee to create a relationship deep in mutual respect, understanding, and genuine interest. This type of connection focuses on the employee and makes her feel cared about, thus increasing your ability to communicate with and influence the employee. Connection at this level brings success to your career.

THE MOST SUCCESSFUL MANAGER

As you can see, if you want to be the **most** successful manager you can be, the kind of manager whose ladder reaches very high, then you have to raise your good communication skills to the level of great connection. Communication is the road, connection is the actual road trip. In other words, if you **use communication to connect** with your employees, you will succeed.

You know people who are successful communicators, but not great connectors. The sage-on-the-stage professor comes to mind. Let's assume the professor is an effective speaker and an outstanding expert in his field. He is able to communicate the information to you in a way that will allow you to pass your test at the end of the class. But this professor will not change your life, will not engage or motivate you. He does not connect with you.

You also know managers who communicate well, but do not know how to truly connect with their employees. In their departments, the employees are most often committed to their paychecks, not the work itself. Because the manager is a good communicator, there are few employee problems or issues that come up between employees or between the manager and employees, but there is also little commitment beyond the obligation of the work. Everything is just "ok."

Now consider the manager who knows how to connect with her employees. Because of her ability to connect, the manager has strong and healthy one-on-one connections with each of her employees. These relationships form the foundation for a great work environment where the employees are engaged with each other and with the work itself, and motivated to do their best work.

To achieve this connection-level communication and become the most successful manager you can be, you need to develop a communication style to get you there. This is where Connect & Succeed comes in.

CONNECT & SUCCEED

Connect & Succeed is an enhanced, high-quality style of communication that will take you from mere communication to connection. It is connection-level communication at its best. It is the kind of connection that leads straight to success.

One of the principles of Connect & Succeed is a focus on your employee as a full person, not just a job title. This focus benefits everyone involved, and is a natural outcome of the first element of Connect & Succeed: Energetic Listening.

The second element is Targeted Speaking, where you let an employee know that he is cared about. In other words, the employee feels like he is heard, respected, and valued. It is a proven way to open up the employee's highest level of work.

The third principle is to connect via common ground, and so, the third element is Common Ground Connection. This style of connection is extremely effective because it is based on establishing common ground between you and each of your employees. This foundation allows for true and open connection in the workplace. This is Connect & Succeed level connection.

For some, making connections with others comes more naturally. If, like me, you are more introverted, you might be experiencing some struggles in your ability to connect. I did. Connect & Succeed can help both the natural and the more introverted communicator learn to connect.

Every manager can benefit from a conscious strategy to enhance her communication style, and every manager can learn how to improve her ability to connect with her employees.

THE CONNECT & SUCCEED CONVERSATION

The Connect & Succeed conversation is the vehicle to connection. It is almost too simple—all managers have conversations with their employees. The one-on-one conversation with an employee is where connection can be most successfully created, and is therefore the touchpoint of Connect and Succeed.

Three important points about the Connect & Succeed conversation:

- The elements of the conversation, listening, speaking, and connecting, weave together during a conversation.
- The face-to-face aspect of a conversation is important.
- It will take time and effort to learn to lead a Connect & Succeed conversation, but it will be worthwhile!

Let's look more closely at each of these points:

LISTENING, SPEAKING, & CONNECTING

Any given conversation is an intricate weave of listening, speaking, and connecting. While Connect & Succeed has Energetic Listening, Targeted Speaking, and Common Ground Connection as separate elements, this is with the full acknowledgement that in real-life conversations, they all mix together.

Specifically, with Connect & Succeed, the weave of Energetic Listening and Targeted Speaking will help you find the common ground to use in creating the Common Ground Connection. They are set up as separate elements in this book because this allows you to look more deeply at each factor.

FACE-TO-FACE

It is in the face-to-face conversation where your Connect & Succeed style comes alive. It is the primary touchpoint for you, and the perfect opportunity to connect with your employees.

In recent years "conversation" has become a buzz word for many global companies looking to bring the face-to-face interaction back into their managerial structures. Companies are realizing that the simple conversation can be highly effective in building trust, engagement, motivation, and commitment among their employees. Furthermore, one-on-one conversations can facilitate strong communication between management levels and employees.

These face-to-face conversations with employees can be formal or informal in nature. You might also find that your face-to-face conversation is via a computer stream or video conferencing. Technology has enlarged our ability to have face-to-face conversations, and no matter the manner, the goal is to use the conversations to improve and/or maintain strong connections with your employees.

TIME AND EFFORT

It is true that both effective connection, and specifically, the use of Connect & Succeed, takes time and effort. If you are a manager and trying to sidestep connection as an integral part of your job, you will always find your job challenging and frequently find yourself behind the eight ball. If instead, you embrace both the need to effectively connect with your employees and the enhancements of the Connect & Succeed communication style, you will find that your time and effort will pay off in spades. It is that simple.

It is also true that you may have a department that has so many employees that having Connect & Succeed conversations with each of them does not seem feasible. Two points here: 1) If you, for instance, create connection with your supervisors, their engagement and motivation will filter down to the employees they supervise, and 2) Remember that once embraced, the Connect & Succeed style allows you to more easily connect. This means that you will not particularly need long, formal conversations with every employee in your department. A simple shared interest in a particular sport may be the common ground that can easily be touched upon with a comment made to an employee you are passing in a hallway. The very fact that you make a quick comment will go a long way in terms of connection.

CONNECT & SUCCEED BENEFITS

While the focus of this book is on engaging and motivating your employees, there are many benefits to adopting a Connect & Succeed communication style in your role as a manager. The benefits land on both sides of your employees, because in addition to improving your relationships with your employees, Connect & Succeed will prosper you, and your department and company. The benefits will be wide-ranging and make a significant impact on your success at your company.

YOUR BENEFITS

Your work and career will be more rewarding and satisfying. Imagine coming to a job everyday where you struggle to get your employees to meet their deadlines and finish their projects. Imagine that they all look at their jobs as obligations they must fulfill to get a paycheck. Imagine feeling that way yourself.

Now imagine walking into your office feeling connected and energized. Because you have great relationships at work, you look forward to coming to the office. You feel respected and effective as a manager. In fact, because of your connection with your employees, they are willing and eager to go the extra mile for you. This second scenario feels leap years ahead of the first scenario, and is the number one reason why you want to adopt a Connect & Succeed style. It feels good!

In your work itself, your personal productivity will jump, your influence with your employees will increase, and you will be seen as a manager who is stepping up in terms of productivity and leadership.

Using Connect and Succeed to connect will bring success. As you move up the ladder of your company, you will find your path supported by the strong connections you have created with the employees on your team. This is a great way to succeed.

YOUR EMPLOYEES

If you want your employees to be productive, you need them to be engaged, and motivated. The best, and really the only way, to create this engagement and motivation in your department is through effective manager–employee connection.

When you connect with your employees you establish the level of manager-employee relationships that powers a department forward. The greatest aspect of this will be the way you power up each of your employees, and the long lasting personal and professional benefits this then gives to them. Yes, benefitting your employees benefits the department itself, but that takes nothing away from the fact that each employee is served.

Let's look more specifically at the ways your employees will benefit from your Connect & Succeed communication style, in terms of engagement and motivation:

ENGAGEMENT

An engaged employee is an employee who feels emotionally linked to his company. This link influences his approach and commitment to his work and aligns him more strongly with the company, and its goals and success.

Obviously, an employee's engagement is a significant factor. Three benefits of your Connect & Succeed style will greatly contribute to your employees' feeling of engagement:

- Increased trust
- Stronger employee development
- Higher employee commitment

INCREASED TRUST

When they experience connection with you, your employees will know you better. This means they are more likely to trust you, and be open to the information you share and the feedback you give.

This trust usually cements in clarity, because a good connection with an employee allows you to be more direct in your directions and expectations. Clarity raises the performance potential and engagement of everyone involved – and as you will learn in this book, clarity is an important benefit of a Connect & Succeed style.

STRONGER EMPLOYEE DEVELOPMENT

Your Connect & Succeed manager-employee relationships will allow you to more easily support and develop your employees. You will know the specific characteristics of each of your employees: Their recognition needs, talents, and challenges. With this information, you will be able to tailor your development of that employee more precisely. You will know how to bring out the best in each person. This kind of employee development will increase your employees' engagement at work.

Your Connect & Succeed style will also help you to develop your employees through an emotional channel, because a Connect & Succeed connection is deep and works on many levels, including emotional levels.

In a Dale Carnegie Training and MSW-ARS Research's study on employee engagement, they found that the evocation of specific emotions such as "enthusiasm, inspiration, empowerment and confidence" would lead to more engagement, and suggests that "Organizations can work to foster these emotions as part of their employee engagement strategy by improving the relationships employees have with managers and senior leaders" (Dale Carnegie Training).

HIGHER EMPLOYEE COMMITMENT

Your commitment to your employees' commitment is part of your Connect & Succeed style. Furthermore, your commitment to them will generate commitment from them, and their overall engagement will rise.

Commitment itself is difficult to measure, but one of the most telling factors around commitment is employee retention. The attrition numbers at a company are solid indicators of your employees' commitment. If a company cannot keep its talented and productive employees, there is a problem.

There are also costs, figurative and literal. High turnover affects the motivation and engagement of the employees who are still there. Literal costs include the recruitment and training of new employees. Every year companies spend a significant amount of money due to employee turnover.

It is simple to see that if you, as the manager, adopt a Connect & Succeed style with your employees, you can head off the factors that cause employees to leave. It will be the connection you have with your employees that will keep your relationships strong. The employees will feel like their current work situation is one where they can thrive, grow, and do their best. They will be committed and therefore, engaged.

MOTIVATION

When your connection with your employees is positive and effective, their motivation will skyrocket. Highly motivated employees are commonly credited with 300-500% more productivity than poorly motivated employees.

Employees' motivation levels are very important to everyone involved. Your connection with your employees will boost their motivation level because the connection will give them:

- A sense of being seen as an individual
- A strong feeling of being supported
- A proactive approach to problem solving

SEEN AS AN INDIVIDUAL

There are, of course, boundaries to your relationships with your employees, and a degree of professionalism is always necessary. Yet because we all spend an incredible amount of our waking hours at our jobs, being seen, respected, and valued on an individual level is a motivating factor for each employee.

As you will learn, the very way a Connect & Succeed conversation is set up, your employee will feel cared about—and this is motivating.

STRONGLY SUPPORTED

In a connected department, your employees will feel supported on both a personal and professional level. When employees feel supported, their motivation will be high. This is what Connect & Succeed is all about.

For instance, as part of your Connect & Succeed conversations, you will be encouraging and praising your employee for her accomplishments and talents. In this way, your employee will be supported over time, and in an authentic and true way. Furthermore, because you have truly connected with your employee, you can tailor the recognition to the individual employee. Consistent and tailored praise in the course of your interactions with the employee will feel good – for you and the employee. This will motivate everyone.

PROACTIVE PROBLEM SOLVING

Being proactive about employee problems is a natural outcome of a Connect & Succeed managerial style. When you, as the manager, have developed real connections with your employees, and continue to improve and maintain these connections, the issue will not be employee problems, but rather, employee problem solving. When employees know that you support them, and when there is a Connect & Succeed "open door" atmosphere, they will come to you with their problems – and this is a good thing.

In a Connect & Succeed department, you can solve problems with your employees as they arise. The best problem solving is fast and timely. In the end, this type of approach will save time and effort. It sure beats quarterly, or even once yearly, performance reviews, and a situation where all the problems have been brewing and piling up for months. Those are not conversations that make you, or the employee, feel good.

YOUR DEPARTMENT & YOUR COMPANY

As executive business coach Patrick Summar points out, "Good communication is the lifeblood of a company. Therefore, if the communication reaches connection level, it will significantly raise the health and performance of that company."

Your Connect & Succeed communication style will resonate beyond you, into your department as a whole, and the company itself. It will show up in the workplace environment, the productivity of your department and the bottom line of your company.

WORKPLACE ENVIRONMENT

When you and your employees are connected, how can your department's workplace environment not be magnetic and potent? I knew a middle manager at a university hospital. The "in" place to be at 7 am each weekday morning was in his office. All of his supervisors were there—even hospital administrators, his bosses, showed up. No official business went on, but the discussions set the stage for the rest of the day.

An added bonus was that all of his employees were there on time, ready to start their work at 8 am. This is how connection works! Compare this to a memo instructing all employees to be on time in response to a lateness issue.

PRODUCTIVITY

Your bottom line as a manager is for your department to be effective and successful in finishing projects by being productive. As a manager, it is your job to coordinate all the moving parts to make this happen. Depending on the situation, there can be lots of moving parts.

Furthermore, at your best, you will need to make the most efficient use of all your resources: Employees, time, materials, etc. Communication is the skill that can make all of this happen. Communication at the level of connection is going to improve your chances of success and make the process easier. It will both provide more traction on the track, and a more powerful fuel for the process.

THE COMPANY'S BOTTOM LINE

The benefit of a Connect & Succeed style is validated by everything from your mother's common sense to proven studies from think tanks and research firms around the world. Your mother knows that if your department is filled with employees who are engaged and motivated, success will be yours. She also knows that those engaged and motivated employees will make your department the place to be within the company. She knows that this will be reflected in your department's productivity. She is particularly pleased that your department's productivity will increase the company's bottom line, and she is therefore happy to know that you will be moving up the success ladder very quickly, and proud of the way you will do this!

CHAPTER TWO

The Connect & Succeed Style

The simple but high-quality enhancements of a Connect & Succeed style will move your conversations from mere communication to successful connections. This means that in the same time it takes you to communicate information to your employees, you can instead connect with them. This means that they will receive the information and instructions you need to communicate while being engaged and motivated to do the work. Each conversation then works on several levels: There is shared information, creation of an inspirational, emotion-based bond, and a mutually beneficial interaction, all elements that make connection real and viable.

Furthermore, the idea of Connect & Succeed as a style is intentional. Instead of seeing it as a new process to add to your work, you will see that once integrated into your communication, it will be a natural and easy way to communicate and connect, rather than an extra task to add to your to-do list.

ELEMENTS OF CONNECTION

As touched on in Chapter One, there are three elements to connection:

- Energetic Listening
- Targeted Speaking
- Common Ground Connection

Each one comes with a deep well of information and skill building.

To develop your Connect & Succeed communication style, you will use this information and skill building to improve and uplevel your ability to connect. With this ability, each conversation you have with an employee will become an opportunity to find common ground and enhance your connection to that employee. Together, these touchpoints will build up your success.

ENERGETIC LISTENING

LISTENING IS KEY

Listening is a very personal activity, whether you realize it or not. Human beings innately desire to be heard. Listening to people is an incredible way to let them know that you are focused on them, and truly up-levels the quality of your relationships. Energetic listening will create benefits that resonate on multiple levels, from individual employees to the company as a whole.

Listening is also important because when an employee is talking, he opens himself up to rejection. We all feel rejected when we are talking and the other person does not seem to be interested in what we have to say. A rejected employee is not an employee at his best, and obviously, this makes it much more difficult to establish common ground connection.

Good listening will show your employees that you are willing to connect with them, and this will encourage them to risk being open in their communication with you. You will create an environment where people are truly willing to contribute to a given project or product. We all know we are at our best when we are not afraid to share our ideas, even the "crazy" ones, which might just lead to more success for everyone.

Also, when you listen to each of your employees, it will become contagious. They will listen to you, and their fellow employees, at the same level. Listening can then become like a virus that spreads. You listen to your employee, she then listens to her colleague, who then listens to his employee... and eventually, everyone in your department feels heard, and that means they will all be better listeners – and listening to you! This openness will allow real collaboration and teamwork, instead of competition and back biting. As a result you will become a more successful manager.

Furthermore, your leadership as a manager will improve because of the trust, respect, and integrity you have shown your employees by listening to them. They will return the trust, respect, and integrity to you.

FOCUS ON THE EMPLOYEE

For some, a conversation is a chance to tell others what they think. In these conversations, the two-way aspect of the conversations gets lost. This is especially possible in work situations between managers and employees: The manager speaks and the employee listens. This one-way conversation is rarely fruitful, unless you run your department as a "my way or the highway" manager. If you do, this book is not for you.

By focusing on the employee in your Connect & Succeed conversation, you will find a full person and be able to see beyond the label of "employee." With this extra "intel" you will be able to better manage that employee. You will know how to engage and motivate him. You will be able to foresee potential problems and take proactive actions. You will understand how to best utilize each employee you manage, which means that your project completion will take care of itself. By listening energetically to your employee, you will see the whole person, find areas of common ground, and be able to establish the type of Connect & Succeed connection that will serve you both.

AN ENHANCED LEVEL

Research tells us that we generally remember 25-50% of what we hear. With energetic listening you aspire to raise this percentage dramatically, and make a conscious choice to not just hear the words your employee says, but to understand the full message she is conveying, and then to use this understanding to establish connection with her.

Energetic Listening is an enhanced style of listening that will make connecting with your employees an easy and effective task. It is an active and attentive form of listening. You listen with an energy for listening.

ENERGETIC LISTENING SKILLS

In order to listen energetically, you need to pay attention, which is easier said than done. Connect & Succeed will show you how to deal with distractions, including the distraction of your own attention span. This will make a big difference in your listening. Further, you will learn techniques to expand your attention span. Finally in paying attention, raising your connection awareness will be an important part of listening energetically.

With Energetic Listening it is also crucial to take note of more than just the verbal part of the conversation. This means you must learn to pinpoint the nonverbal signals from the other person.

The key is to develop the ability to do all of these things in a fluid and integrated way, so that they can be done as an active and natural part of the conversation.

TARGETED SPEAKING

SPEAKING TO CONNECT

A conversation where you only listen is one-way, and can be as ineffective as the conversation where you only speak. A conversation is, at its best, an interaction that connects the two people involved.

Of course, as a manager you will use some of your speaking time to share information, give instructions, set goals, review projects and performance, etc. but you also want to use your speaking time for Targeted Speaking, which is about speaking to connect. On one hand, this means for you to speak with clarity and in a way that tailors your message, adapts your speaking style, and highlights the common ground between you and the specific employee you are interacting with.

Target Speaking is also about supporting the speaker as he speaks. You support the speaker by actively acknowledging the speaker, both verbally and nonverbally. You also spotlight the common ground between you as the employee speaks. Finally, you deal with disagreement in a Connect & Succeed way – which is to say, that while you acknowledge and face any disagreements, you also continue to support the employee. In this way, disagreement does not dissolve into bigger problems, but instead keeps the door open to connection.

Ultimately, Targeted Speaking supports and encourages your employee to fully participate in the conversation by validating both who the employee is and what that employee is saying. Targeted Speaking with an employee is especially important because as the employee's manager, you are automatically in a leadership position in the conversation. This can create the type of unequal footing that can get in the way of connection. On one hand, you want to be respected for your position as manager, but on the other hand, you don't want the employee to hold back in a way that closes down connection. By taking a leadership role in the conversation and using Targeted Speaking to support and encourage the speaker, you can balance everything out, and increase your chances of successful connection.

CARE ABOUT THE EMPLOYEE

Each conversation, formal or informal, long or short, planned or spontaneous, can be an opportunity to connect, and that simple act of connection can make your employees feel heard, respected, and valued, and therefore, cared about. When your employees feel cared about, they will be the kind of employees who bring energy and passion to their work. As a Dale Carnegie study tells us: "Employees who reported that their managers care about their personal lives are 3x more engaged than those that do not believe that" (Dale Carnegie Training).

I grew up in the Midwest, and it is common as you walk neighborhoods or downtown streets to nod and say hello to people you pass, whether you know them or not. I did not realize how significant this simple connection could be until I moved to bigger cities where you might easily pass someone on the street without any connection. In fact, some people purposely look away and scuttle by. Translate this into a work environment and passing your employees in the hallways. It is minor, but on a human level, you can see how these encounters could make an employee feel unseen and uncared for.

Instead, think about how it feels to be heard, respected, and valued. Imagine if your employees felt this from you. Imagine how much more engaged and motivated they would be. Imagine how this would make your effectiveness as a manager easier to accomplish.

With Connect & Succeed, your Targeted Speaking will make the task of caring about your employees, by supporting and encouraging them, easy and natural. Every conversation you have with an employee will be building up a bank account of "heard, respected, and valued."

AN ENHANCED LEVEL

In your conversation with an employee, Targeted Speaking is an enhanced use of speaking aimed at inspiring the employee to truly open to a connection with you. Targeted Speaking relates to how you verbally participate in the conversation and respond to what the other person says. Inspiring your employee to connect with you is what drives your Targeted Speaking.

TARGETED SPEAKING SKILLS

There are two sides of the coin to Targeted Speaking: One is for you to speak with clarity out of respect for the employee you are interacting with. This clarity is not just centered around you saying what you want to say, but takes into account how well the employee is understanding the meaning you want to convey. You are targeting your speaking because you care about the employee.

You clarify what you say by tailoring your message to the person you are having the conversation with. You also consider your speaking style in general, and enhance it for the best possible communication and connection possibilities. Finally, you highlight the common ground as you speak. In other words, you speak of the common ground you share with your employee.

The second side to the coin uses your Targeted Speaking to support the employee as she speaks. You can support the speaker by actively acknowledging what she is saying, in both verbal and nonverbal ways. Additionally, as you support the speaker, you can also target your speaking to spotlight the common ground. Finally, in support of the speaker, you want to deal with any disagreements in a Connect & Succeed style. You can allow disagreements to be aired in a conversation, while keeping them from derailing the connection itself.

Overall, when you use your Targeted Speaking to show a curiosity about what is being said, an openness to whatever point of view and opinions the employee has to share, and a real desire to hear what the employee can contribute to the conversation, you are succeeding. All of this, and more, can be done with the right Targeted Speaking skills.

COMMON GROUND CONNECTION

THE SPARK OF CONNECTION

The actual experience of connection is bigger than any definition of the term. You know exactly what it feels like when you have connected with someone. There is a spark to the connection. You feel congruent and in alignment with the other person. It is a great win-win feeling, and creates the groundwork for a work relationship that will prosper both of you.

Specifically, when you connect with an employee, you will feel the mutual respect. You can definitely be at different levels within a company's managerial structure, but have a balanced respect for each other. When you connect with an employee, it makes it easier to rally around the same project or company objective. Having your employees work with you, not against or in other directions, is success itself.

COMMON GROUND

Common ground is the place where something about you—your ideas, stories, interests, personality, viewpoints, background, preferences, idiosyncrasies, etc.—intersects and overlaps with something about the person you are talking to. When you have common ground with your employees, you essentially have a foundation of mutual understanding. This foundation allows true and open communication, aka connection.

Interestingly enough, common ground can unite people with divergent views even if the common ground is not about the subject you are discussing. For instance, you and your employee might disagree on a given project choice, but still speak from a place of common ground because you both have the same overall career goals.

Remember that common ground is based on understanding, not just on agreement. Ideally, you can disagree on a particular topic and still find common ground. An obvious example here is a situation where you are both fans of a college football team, but they are rival teams. The common ground is the love of college football teams. This same type of common ground can be found with more work-related issues. Your employee may not be a supporter of the new CEO, but you feel very excited about the changes that this CEO is bringing. You and your employee still share the common ground of wanting both your department to shine in the next quarter, and wanting the company to do well overall, so that both of your jobs stay secure.

FIND COMMON GROUND

For most of us, finding common ground with some people is easy, and with others more difficult. Either way, begin with the first step.

Sally Patchen, a mediator and strategic negotiation consultant, is an expert in finding common ground. In her work, she is often seeking common ground with parties that have already made conscious steps away from each other. She wisely notes that "Common ground is established when you can find just one thing that you can agree upon." She is successful in her work because she can take that one thing and use it as both a "starting point" and "a safe place to return to" when needed.

As you begin your search for common ground, be willing to treasure the smallest parcel of shared ground. Common ground is so potent that even the smallest amount can improve the chances of making a connection.

As your connection with a given employee moves forward, you will be able to build on the initial treasure. You can also see how the first two elements of Connect & Succeed, Energetic Listening and Targeted Speaking, will continue to unearth common ground treasures.

CONNECT THROUGH COMMON GROUND

To connect through common ground you use the common ground you found through your Energetic Listening and

Targeted Speaking. You use the common ground to create a path to connection.

Notice that, as the manager, it is important for you to take the lead in acknowledging the common ground. You energetically listen for it and target your speaking to share your desire to work from a place of common ground. In this way, you open and deepen the connection.

Remember that the rewards of Connect & Succeed communication and the finding and establishing of common ground are not distinct from each other because your Energetic Listening, Targeted Speaking, and Common Ground Connection are all layered together in a way that makes the "work" of connection a process you can enjoy and benefit from. Interestingly, because of the weave of conversations, you connect as you pursue the process of connection.

Finding common ground in your communication with employees will transform walls into bridges. It will remove barriers between you and your employees. By connecting with your employees at a common ground level, you empower your relationship with them. And as you know, this simple relationship can build powerful success at any company.

YOUR CONNECT & SUCCEED STRATEGY

Having a strategy for the implementation of your Connect & Succeed style will up your game considerably.

This starts with the right preparation. Raising your communication style to a new level means that things will change, both within and around you – and being ready for this change is important.

As part of this preparation, you want to set your goals and timeline. Both of these items will motivate and guide you as you move forward.

Finally, you will want to keep track of both your progress and your connections. In keeping track you will assess, reflect, and take notes. This is a key part of your Connect & Succeed Strategy because it gives you a solid foundation from which you will continue to succeed.

USING THIS BOOK

Communication alone is a complex subject. Connection-level communication adds to it. This is why you have been tipped off to the fact that the skills and topics covered in this book are ultimately meant to flow together into a fluid real-life conversation. Yet, in order to go into each topic in an in-depth and complete way, the elements of Connect & Succeed are broken down into their parts.

This is then a reminder that you will not be able to do everything all at once. This book is rich in skills, information, and exercises – and is best digested over time. Specifically, since the topics are broken down into chapters, then sections, you might want to work with one section at a time. This will allow you to dive deeply into that topic, and give you the focus to absorb the information and build your skills.

Also note that some topics and themes will be repeated in different sections of the book. They are repeated on purpose—to highlight how the topic is relevant from several angles when discussing communication and connection. For example, emotional contagion is discussed twice, once from an Energetic Listening angle, and again from a Targeted Speaking angle.

Chapter 8 is about your Connect & Succeed strategy. There is a section there that deals with your readiness to transition to a Connect & Succeed style. If you have any hesitations as you enter this journey, check out Chapter 8 now.

Chapter 8 also gives you some instructions on putting together a Connect & Succeed Operating Manual. The operating manual gives you a place to keep your notes from completed Connect & Succeed exercises. Furthermore, once you have done an exercise, you are encouraged to create both some standard procedures for your unique process and keep track of your successes and connections.

My suggestion is to read the book through once, knowing you will be returning to it again and again, because as you connect, you will succeed, and you will therefore want to come back to this book for another step up your success ladder.

II.
ENERGETIC LISTENING

CHAPTER THREE

Pay Attention

Most of us are guilty of multi-tasking. When one of the tasks you are juggling is a conversation, there are big consequences. Now think about a conversation where you are speaking and the other person is not paying attention. No connection is being created, and communication is barely, or not at all, hitting its mark.

Paying attention to the employee you are interacting with makes a huge impact on your ability to listen energetically. It sounds like something your mother or teacher told you back in second grade. Or you simply believe you already know all about paying attention. Yes, it is easy to acknowledge the importance of paying attention, but it is a far cry from using this powerful skill to upgrade to your Connect & Succeed style.

There are many obstacles between knowing that listening with attention is important, and doing it with your employees on a consistent basis. For one thing, your ability to deal with distractions is important because in almost every workplace there will be distractions, and they will interfere with your goal of focusing on the other person during your conversation. If you have a strategy for dealing with distractions, they will be less distracting.

Expanding your attention span is also a crucial skill to master. Being aware of your attention span is a good start. Beyond this, you can use a strategy that will expand your current attention span. Connect & Succeed managers have wise control of their attention spans.

Finally, in order to listen with attention in a Connect & Succeed way, you will raise your connection aptitude by both increasing your self-awareness and learning to listen for the subtle meanings behind the literal verbal meaning.

Listening with attention will totally open your path to success. This Connect & Succeed skill is evaporating into dust in our current society—and if you have it, you will truly stand out as a manager. In fact, you will be appreciated by both your employees and your employers.

Since the ability to focus and pay attention to someone is a key component of Energetic Listening, we will now dive more deeply into how to:

- Deal With Distractions
- Expand Your Attention Span
- Raise Your Connection Awareness

DEAL WITH DISTRACTIONS

DISTRACTION PREVENTION

Your goal is to be fully present in your energetic listening, so distractions can be a big problem. Yet most workplace situations are filled with a large assortment of distraction possibilities. External distractions such as other conversations going on around you, noise from an office or nearby machinery, incoming phone calls... and the list goes on. Additionally, there are the internal distractions like hunger or fatigue.

The common denominator about distractions is that they are the enemies of energetic listening because they actively try to grab your attention.

ELIMINATE THE DISTRACTION

When you face distractions, the most obvious action is to eliminate the distraction. If for example, you are trying to communicate with someone in a noisy place, go someplace where it is quieter. If you are feeling a mid-afternoon energy slump, take a short walk before your conversation. In these cases, staying fully focused will be easier thanks to these simple remedies.

BE PROACTIVE

Notice that being proactive about identifying the potential

distractions ahead of time can make your energetic listening easier from the start. For instance, you might ask someone to pick up your phone line while you are having an important conversation with one of your employees. To anticipate distractions ask yourself: "What might cause me to lose focus?" Do you need to turn off your cell phone, log off the internet, forward your calls, or close your office door? Are there too many people coming into your office with questions or concerns? Being aware of these and other distractions ahead of time will help you create meaningful Connect & Succeed conversations.

WORK WITH A DISTRACTION

If you cannot remove the distraction, acknowledge it and work with the employee to have a successful conversation despite the distraction. You might also find ways to deal with the distraction(s). As an example, if there are lots of other people talking around you, it would be tempting to look around while you are talking to your employee. Instead, you can concentrate on maintaining eye contact with the person you are talking with, keeping your connection intact.

MANAGE THE EMPLOYEE

Dealing with distractions can also mean managing the employee you are connecting with. For example, if the other person is really excited about something and is talking too fast, ask him to slow down so that you can really connect with what he is saying. By taking charge of your conversations in this way, you are using Energetic Listening in the most effective way.

<u>PREPARE</u>

You can also help yourself fully focus by getting mentally ready before a conversation. That means making a mental decision to fully focus on a particular conversation to the exclusion of everything else. As much as possible, put everything out of your mind, so that you have "room" to fully focus on the other person and the information she is sharing. This mental clarity and commitment helps you focus your energetic listening.

EXERCISE 1: DISTRACTION PREVENTION

- List common external distractions in your office and workplace.

- Next to each external distraction listed, write down 1-2 ways to remove or reduce the distraction.

- List common internal distractions you experience while in your office and workplace.

- Next to each internal distraction listed, write down 1-2 ways to remove or reduce the distraction.

- For the external distractions, take a proactive approach to removing or reducing the distractions you have identified. This might involve extra preparation for any given conversation.

- For the internal distractions, prepare yourself to be fully focused. Deal with your internal distractions ahead of the conversation.

- As you implement these distraction prevention methods, keep track of what works and what does not work.

EXPAND YOUR ATTENTION SPAN

Maintaining your attention and full focus as part of your energetic listening is often difficult because of the challenges of your attention span. The human attention span is only 3-24 seconds, with the average at about 12 seconds. That means while you are trying to focus, your attention is constantly wandering off, then coming back to the conversation at hand. In most instances you do this in fractions of a second, so you can still carry on a conversation and maintain your energetic listening.

The real problem occurs when you "wander off," but do not come back to the conversation in which you are engaged. You actually shift your focus to something else, and your energetic listening is disrupted. When this happens, you effectively tune out the other person and break down any connection you have established.

It does not make the other person feel very good when they realize you are no longer listening, and in most cases, the other person can tell when you are daydreaming or "off somewhere" during a conversation. You can't hide the glassy-eyed look that indicates your body is there, but your mind is not.

When you do not face your attention span challenges you are diminishing your chances of being a successful Connect & Succeed manager. You are not doing something that is essential in your job—listening energetically to the people who report to you.

ATTENTION SPAN STRATEGIES

There are three Connect & Succeed strategies to help you deal with your attention span challenges:

- Accept that your mind will wander, but counter this natural tendency with a stronger and stronger ability to refocus quickly.
- Train yourself for longer attention spans.
- Use techniques during the conversation that will lengthen your attention span.

REFOCUS QUICKLY
EXERCISE 2: CREATE A TRIGGER

Use a physical trigger to bring you quickly back to your Connect & Succeed conversation:

- Create the trigger by role-playing or imagining a situation where your mind wanders during a conversation.

- As you come back into a full presence in the conversation, make the physical movement or gesture that you want to use as a trigger. This physical movement or gesture will be the trigger for your state of full presence and energetic listening.

- Common discreet triggers include: Wiggling your toes or holding your thumb and index fingertip together.

- Train yourself to this trigger by repeating the above steps until the trigger triggers itself.

- Test your trigger in real life conversations. The more you use it, the stronger the trigger.

TRAIN YOURSELF FOR LONGER ATTENTION SPANS

EXERCISE 3: POWER HOURS

Practice the use of Power Hours as an exercise to increase your attention span:

- Decide on the task you will focus on and set a timer for 50 minutes.

- Make an agreement with yourself that for those 50 minutes you will focus exclusively on that one task.

- At the end of the 50 minutes, celebrate your success for 10 minutes: Take a break, stretch, take a walk...

Because you may not be able to take a whole hour for one task, you can easily break the power hours down to power half-hours or power ten minutes.

This practice will not only increase your personal productivity, but also increase your attention span when energetically listening to your employees.

EXERCISE 4: MEDITATION

Meditation teaches you to focus your attention for longer and longer periods of time. Your goal is to increase your attention span, which will be beneficial overall, as well as in your energetic listening.

- Sit in a comfortable position, paying attention to your posture and breathing. Your goal is a relaxed but alert state of mind.

- Bring your hands together in a prayer position in front of your body at chest level.

- Close your eyes.

- Press the tips of your middle fingers gently together and focus your attention there.

- If you focus wanders away, gently bring it back to the spot where your middle fingers are pressing together.

- Continue to practice this meditation daily. You will notice that your ability to focus will increase, and that your mind will wander less and less.

USE ATTENTION SPAN TECHNIQUES DURING THE CONVERSATION

EXERCISE 5: ATTENTION SPAN TECHNIQUES

Use the following techniques during your conversations:

- Focus on hearing each word the speaker is saying. This will help you stay engaged in your energetic listening.

- Keep your eye contact with the speaker active and steady. Paying attention to what you are seeing will help you to stay alert and tuned into what is being said.

- Keep track of how successful you are with these techniques.

RAISE YOUR CONNECTION AWARENESS

Since connection is your goal, as you listen you will find that both the act of energetic listening itself, and the information gleaned from listening with so much attention, will contribute to the connection you are creating with your employee. It follows then that the more aware you are in your Energetic Listening, the more connection that can be made.

As an Energetic Listener, there are two areas around awareness that you want to sharpen:

1. Your self-awareness – because the more you understand your own thoughts, emotions, needs, desires, beliefs, and attitudes, the more open you will be to others.

2. Your ability to pick up the subtle meanings behind your employee's spoken words.

INCREASE YOUR SELF-AWARENESS

For the purposes of Connect & Succeed, self-awareness is understanding yourself within the context of a conversation – in particular, in how you pay attention. Being self-aware is relevant before, during, and after the actual conversation.

Essentially, the more comfortable you are with yourself, the more clarity you will bring to the conversation, and the more open you will be to the employee. From the other direction, the employee will pick up on your ability to be genuine in the conversation, as well as feeling the "invitation" to also be authentic. In this way, the environment of the conversation is very conducive to connection.

The great thing is that you can use the Connect & Succeed conversation itself to increase your self-awareness. Through the close listening of Energetic Listening, you will be able to learn things about yourself, by both what is said to you and by how you respond. Be open to this continuing education.

EXERCISE 6: YOUR SELF-AWARENESS

A surprisingly short pause for a post-conversation reflection can offer great insights:

- Take five-ten minutes after your conversation with an employee to reflect upon what you learned about yourself from the conversation.

- Write down anything that you learned about your thoughts, emotions, needs, desires, beliefs, and/or attitudes.

- Remember to reflect on not just what you said, but also what you heard from your employee, and your responses to what your employee said. All aspects of the conversation are potential goldmines for a deeper understanding of yourself.

DETECT SUBTLE MEANINGS

Particularly in manager-employee conversations, an employee could speak more cautiously or indirectly. As your connection gets stronger, this will be less of a problem, but it is also important for you to take the lead on listening on a level where you can hear the subtle messages embedded in the context of what is being said.

To pick up the subtle meanings, you will want to tune in as you listen. Specifically, you will tune into:

- Both the tone of the verbal message and the language the speaker chooses.
- What is not being said.
- The underlying emotions of what your employee is saying.

In these ways, you truly enhance the level of attention you are bringing to your listening.

TONE AND LANGUAGE

Tuning in involves the verbal message you are listening to, but goes beyond the words themselves. This is about listening to the tone of the voice and the language choices used by your employee. Both are big "tells" about the full message being communicated.

TONE

Some define the tone of the voice as a nonverbal factor, but it is also worth its own focus. The tone of the voice includes its quality, pitch, volume, and style. Your voice can reveal a lot about you. Think about how you can hear joy or stress or bravado in a voice. There are times when the tone of the voice is so strong, that it almost does not matter what the person is saying.

There are also situations where the actual meaning of the verbal message is changed completely by the tone in which the message is delivered. When discussing a departmental change, a simple and seemingly "Ok, I agree," can be delivered in a friendly and agreeable tone or in a reluctant and aggressive tone.

For example, consider Mike. When I discussed a departmental policy change with him, he voiced his support of the change in a very neutral tone. Because of my energetic listening skills, I noticed that his tone did not match what he said. I took note of this.

LANGUAGE

I also noticed that Mike seemed to be choosing his words of support very carefully. In fact, because I was paying attention, I realized he had worded his support in a way that gave him an out later: "Ok, I agree, because it doesn't seem that we have any real choice here." This is just one example of how language choices and phrasing can be used. For whatever reason, Mike did not want to reveal his disagreement with the plan, but he really did not want to agree either.

EXERCISE 7: TONE AND LANGUAGE

It is sometimes difficult to trust a "feeling" or hunch that there is a hidden meaning afoot, especially in the face of a verbal statement. Paying close attention to the subtle meanings in tone and language will help you to verify your hunch.

• As you listen to your employee, ask yourself how you would characterize her tone. Then ask yourself if it matches what she is saying. Take note of any discrepancies between the verbal message and the tone used by the speaker. If there are discrepancies, ask yourself if the message or the tone is more accurate?

• As you listen to your employee, ask yourself how you would characterize her language choices. Is there anything in her choice of words that makes you feel like there are several ways to interpret what she is saying? What is the predominant message you hear from her language choices?

• Your consideration of your employee's tone and language will be going on during your conversation. Additionally, you can take some time after the conversation to further reflect on these factors.

WHAT IS NOT BEING SAID

In picking up on a speaker's subtle meanings, another factor to consider, is what is not being said. What is not said can be at least as important, or sometimes more important, than what is said. In many situations, if the employee is leaving things out of the conversation, you are not getting the full message. Connection is critical to your success as a manager, and if an employee feels like there is any reason not to say something he considers relevant, it could become an obstacle to connection.

EXERCISE 8: WHAT IS NOT BEING SAID

- As you listen to your employee, ask yourself if you feel like there is anything your employee is afraid to say to you.

- As you listen to your employee, ask yourself if you feel like there is anything the employee is forgetting to say to you.

- As you listen to your employee, ask yourself if you feel like there is anything the employee is deliberately not telling you.

UNDERLYING EMOTIONS

Often, the emotions behind what your employee is saying are more important than the actual content. This is why you must develop a way to understand the emotions behind what is being said, both consciously through a sensitivity to this layer of the conversation, and naturally, through emotional contagion, which is the natural ripple effect of emotions spreading between people.

SENSITIVITY TO EMOTIONS

When you monitor the emotional impact of a conversation, you are essentially tracking the emotional tenor of what is being said. This is critical for understanding the full scope of what your employee is saying.

An employee might say, "I really enjoy working on this project." If you take their statement literally you would conclude that she really liked the project. If you pick up on the subtle messages, you might learn that she is just saying what she thinks she has to say. You might figure this out because of the lack of enthusiasm in her voice.

Employees hide their true feelings from you for a variety of reasons. By paying attention as part of your Connect & Succeed style, you are tuned into this hidden feeling. This is an important skill because you can imagine how a hidden feeling like this could become an employee problem down the line.

When you allow yourself to be influenced and affected by your employees through an understanding of the emotional backdrop to what they are saying, you are using your sensitivity to emotions in a powerful and conscious way.

To develop the ability to tune into the emotions your employee is feeling, you need to develop a sensitivity that allows you to feel the emotions of your employees. This sensitivity is activated quite simply, by your decision to allow yourself to tune in at this level. This means you must be willing to be affected by what they are feeling.

EXERCISE 9: DEVELOP A STRONGER SENSITIVITY

Sensitivity starts with awareness, and is increased by an openness to new information.

- As you listen to your employee, choose an emotion to define the feeling you sense coming from the employee.

- Ask yourself if the emotion and the verbal message match.

- As you listen, continue to acknowledge not only what is being said, but also the emotions that lie behind the words.

- As with your employee's tone and language, you will be tuning into the employee's emotion during the conversation itself. Additionally, you can reflect further after the conversation.

USE EMOTIONAL CONTAGION TO TUNE IN

Another emotional sensitivity tool that will come in handy is emotional contagion. There is a natural sharing of emotions when two people interact. In other words, the emotions one person feels is contagious to the people this person interacts with. If your employee is feeling a certain emotion, you will naturally find yourself starting to feel the same emotion. If someone is feeling happy, his happiness will be contagious and you will find yourself feeling happier. The flip of the coin is that when a person is unhappy, you will often begin to feel unhappy too. So if you begin to feel an emotion, check in, because it might be telling you what your employee is feeling.

In one of my seminars a manager shared how she was affected by an employee: Every time she had a meeting with this particular employee she ended up feeling depressed. This did not make any sense, because the employee seemed happy. Finally, after a late afternoon meeting with this employee, she went home and her husband asked her why she was so depressed. It hit her. She knew exactly where she had "picked up" the feeling of depression. The next day, in a very professional way, she broached the topic of how the employee was feeling, and found out that he was getting divorced and putting on a happy face to the world. This turned out to be a win-win situation, because while the actual personal topics of depression and divorce were not addressed further, the employee felt cared about, the manager was less confused and able to make productive allowances for this employee, and the connection between them deepened. In fact, the employee felt so supported, that six months later when he was offered a transfer to another department, he stayed with this manager instead.

EXERCISE 10: EMOTIONAL CONTAGION

Identifying the emotions you feel when listening to an employee, could be a window into the employee's feelings. This could be valuable information as you look to connect and succeed.

- As you listen to your employee, identify what emotions you are feeling.

- Note any emotions that might be coming from the conversation, not from within you.

- With this heightened awareness, you will be

able to identify the emotion as either coming from the employee as an emotional contagion or as your own emotion.

• Understanding the emotions behind what your employee is saying will energize your listening.

CHAPTER FOUR

Pinpoint the Nonverbals

Of course, a large part of Energetic Listening is a close and attentive listening to what your employee says. But Energetic Listening is also a "listening" beyond the contents of the message itself. There is lots being said in nonverbal ways, and in order to connect, you will want to be able to tune into all of it.

Specifically, this chapter will show you how to pinpoint the nonverbal physical signals that your employee will give you as she speaks. This involves the identification and translation of the nonverbal signals, as well as the organization of the gathered information into clusters and baselines, and finally, being able to pinpoint the information into useful and valuable knowledge.

Nonverbal pinpointing is an important part of Energetic Listening, and will enhance your ability to listen at the Connect & Succeed level.

NONVERBAL COMMUNICATION

You have been in conversations where your employee is saying one thing verbally, but indicating to you in multiple physical ways that he believes the opposite. For instance, the employee who claims to be confident and 100% on board with a project, but will not look you in the eyes and spends the whole conversation fidgeting with his pen. The verbal message does not seem to match the nonverbal physical message.

Verbal communication is what the employee says. Nonverbal communication includes all the other ways a person can communicate, including her use of facial expressions, eye contact, touch, personal space, clothing, time, and even scent. A simple example here is an employee who shows up to a meeting with a "depressed" body language of slouched shoulders and a bowed head, instead of an energized posture of walking in with her head and shoulders held high. A lot is "said" before any words are spoken.

Add in the fact that it is going on all the time, and you will see that nonverbal communication is a huge and complex topic that can't be ignored. Statistics can vary greatly from conversation to conversation, but studies show that as much as 70-90% of the meaning conveyed in a conversation is nonverbal. The most definitive thing that can be said is that in any conversation, nonverbal signals always convey a significant amount of the meaning.

You are, consciously or not, already picking up on the nonverbal signals of the people you talk and interact with. For instance, when in conversation with an employee you naturally notice if he is looking engaged and interested in what you are saying. This might translate from his alert and forward-leaning posture, or his consistent eye contact with you, or even the smile of agreement on his face. If he looks bored and slumped down, avoids looking at you, and waves his hand in disinterest, you will recognize that this conversation is not hitting the mark! With your Connect & Succeed communication style, you will be more conscious of your ability to recognize the nonverbal communication from your employees.

Ironically, this enhancement will also bring with it a problem: What to do with the now avalanche-sized amount of nonverbal data that you will be able to collect. This is where pinpointing comes in. This allows you to use all the nonverbal data you can collect, but not get overwhelmed by it.

NONVERBAL SIGNALS ARE COMPLEX

Each category of nonverbal communication is complex on its own. As an example, look at the category of facial expression: For those who study this field, there are 21 different facial expressions and seven basic emotions that are expressed. The emotions are surprise, fear, disgust, contempt, anger, sadness, and happiness. Naturally, combinations of these seven must also be factored in.

Now add in the fact that in any given conversation, you will witness an endless stream of facial expressions on the person you are talking to, and some of them will only last for a split second.

This is a lot of complex data to process, and this is just one category of nonverbal communication. Meanwhile, many other nonverbal signals are being sent at the same time!

With verbal communication, you talk, listen, then talk again. With nonverbal communication, the flow is continuous. You are constantly sending and receiving nonverbal signals, whether you intend to or not. Just standing silently in one place communicates to those around you.

MANY MEANINGS

Additionally, each nonverbal signal communicates a broad range of potential meanings, which means that the translation from nonverbal signal to verbal meaning can be intricate, ambiguous, and difficult to understand. Yet the translation is an important part of Connect & Succeed.

The complexity of this is best illustrated with some simple examples:

- In the example mentioned earlier, of the employee who says he is 100% on board with a project, his lack of eye contact could indicate that he is not really on board at all, or it could indicate that he is uncomfortable with you, his manager.
- An employee might be crossing her arms through the conversation and you might translate this as not being

open to your proposal to her. In reality, she may just be physically cold and naturally folding her arms in response to the temperature.

- A smile from your employee might mean agreement, or if his background is from a different culture, the smile may indicate a willingness to keep discussing the matter.

IS IT WORTHWHILE?

So... to be an Energetic Listener you are going to make a conscious effort to identify the nonverbal signals from the employee you are talking to. Then you will go through the complex task of deciphering the meaning of each of his nonverbals signals. You will end up with a large amount of data... and you are beginning to feel the overwhelm of this. No worries.

Let's change your point of view and add in pinpointing to this scenario:

As an Energetic Listener you are able to not only hear what your employee says, but also tune into the nonverbal signals he is communicating to you. Once identified and translated into meaning, you will have a treasure trove of information to use, and once you pinpoint this data you will have valuable and accurate information that will make connecting with this employee an easy bulls-eye.

Furthermore, as your nonverbal pinpointing skills improve, your ability to connect and succeed in style, will be even more meaningful and successful. Yes, this is a very worthwhile skill to learn.

PINPOINTING STEPS

Nonverbal pinpointing is a filtering process. You will take the nonverbal data you have collected during the course of your conversation, and determine what is relevant and essential for a deeper understanding of your employee. This Energetic Listening skill will improve the potential of connection exponentially.

There are three basic steps to pinpointing:

- Identify and Translate the Nonverbal Signals
- Use Clusters and Baselines
- Pinpoint the Nonverbal Signals

Again, as all of the processes in this book, this process has been broken down into steps, but once learned, this can be easily integrated into your conversations in a natural and efficient way.

ONE: IDENTIFY AND TRANSLATE THE NONVERBAL SIGNALS

IDENTIFY

Once you start to be aware of the nonverbal signals given in a conversation, you will not be able to not notice them. For one thing, they are interesting "tells" that can be very revealing.

For this first step, it is important to bring a consciousness to the process. As mentioned, you already naturally notice at least some nonverbal signals, but now you want to improve your ability to "catch them."

TRANSLATE

As you translate a nonverbal signal to a conscious meaning, you need to be cognizant of a few things:

- First, the context of the nonverbal signal.
- Second, the potential nonverbal stereotypes you could slide into.

Also, it is important to make sure your translations are not written in stone. Keep them flexible so that as situations and the employees themselves change, you are not using out-dated viewpoints to translate their nonverbal signals.

CONSIDER CONTEXT

When translating a nonverbal signal you must always consider the context in which it occurs. If one of your employees is crying at the office, you might be concerned. This nonverbal signal that is often associated with sadness is not one you regularly see in the workplace. But if you see this same employee at a funeral for a work colleague, you will not unduly worry if she is crying. The context matches the nonverbal action.

AVOID NONVERBAL STEREOTYPING

Don't be lazy in your translation work. Consider individual employee differences, such as personality factors, gender and cultural differences, etc. By factoring these things in, and not relying on stereotypes, you will be more likely to make an accurate translation. This then improves your chances of connecting with the employee.

Let's look at these factors more closely:

PERSONALITY FACTORS

Clearly the personalities of your employees greatly impacts how they communicate nonverbally. Personality factors that will shift your translation include:

- The openness, curiosity, and creativity of the employee.
- The conscientiousness, self-discipline, and organization of the employee.
- The employee's degree of introversion or extroversion.
- The agreeableness, compassion and cooperative nature of the employee.
- The emotional mindset of the employee, including how he handles anger and anxiety.

For example, an employee who is an extrovert might be more likely to use big gestures and have more animated facial expressions. She might also feel much more comfortable standing close to you. Meanwhile, an introvert might avoid eye contact, maintain a more neutral facial expression, and stand at a distance from you. These nonverbal signals are all related to this individual employee, and if swept up into your translation concerning your connection with the employee, they could lead to a "false positive"–the key word being false.

GENDER DIFFERENCES

There are broad generalizations about how people of different genders express themselves nonverbally. It is fine to acknowledge these, but do not rely on them. Also, make sure you are not falling into gender stereotypes without even realizing that you are doing it. As you translate the nonverbal signals an employee gives you, see that employee as a unique individual.

CULTURAL DIFFERENCES

Factoring in cultural difference can be a good thing, as long as it does not spill over into stereotyping and "lazy" translation. Touch is a great example of how norms can vary from culture to culture. For some, public and casual touching is a comfortable way to interact with work colleagues. For others, even a handshake is not something they are comfortable with.

EXERCISE 11:
IDENTIFY & TRANSLATE NONVERBAL SIGNALS

As with most of the Connect & Succeed skills, you can use them during the conversation, and you can use them after the conversation, in your reflection upon the conversation. This exponentially increases your ability to create connection with your employees.

In the case of identifying and translating the nonverbal signals, doing this both during and after the conversation is most fruitful. The exercise will describe the process during the conversation, but is essentially the same process used after the conversation as a reflection process.

- Notice the nonverbal signals the employee is sending during the conversation.

- Add your translations of his nonverbal signals into verbal meanings. Take context into consideration, and avoid stereotyping.

- Note if and where his verbal messages and nonverbal meanings are congruent, and where they are not.

- If not congruent, note whether it is his words or nonverbal signals which seem to reflect his true thoughts and feelings.

Note that whatever you believe to be his true beliefs or feelings, may not be a black or white issue. He may believe or feel several things at once and it is that conflict that showed up in the conversation. Furthermore, your assessment of the meaning may be inaccurate.

What this exercise and the use of all of the Connect & Succeed skills gives you is someplace to work from. Don't forget that the ultimate goal is not to investigate or study your employee, but rather to find the best ways to connect with him.

TWO: USE CLUSTERS & BASELINES

Generally, if you use only one nonverbal signal in determining the meaning of an employee's communication, your chances of being off track are significant. You are basing it on too little information. This then throws everything about your Energetic Listening off the rail too.

CLUSTERING

For more accurate nonverbal pinpointing, use a technique called clustering. By clustering together the employee's nonverbal signals you will get a clearer picture. It makes sense—several nonverbal signals that indicate the same thing about an employee, increase the likelihood that your translation of her nonverbal signals is on target.

For instance: One of my coaching clients related this story about his employee Patricia. When he talked to Patricia about the company's required overtime for the next month, he noticed that Patricia grimaced. It would be easy to translate that grimace into an assumption that Patricia did not want to do overtime next month. Instead of making this assumption, he continued to energetically listen to Patricia. When she noticed that Patricia's body took on a slouch and, at one point, Patricia made a particular gesture with her hand, my client clustered these signals together and made a more solid determination that Patricia was not happy about the overtime. He later confirmed this assessment.

This clustering, whether done in your head or written down, will make your pinpointing of the nonverbal signals easier. There are two things about the size of the cluster: The bigger the cluster, the more likely it is that it rings true for the employee, even if it contradicts what is being said. Also, the bigger cluster indicates that what lies behind the meaning of the nonverbal signals is important to the employee.

EXERCISE 12: CLUSTERING NONVERBALS

- As you listen to your employee, note the various nonverbal signals he is sending.

- As you translate them, notice how some might reinforce the others, and others might contradict.

- Cluster this information into groups and take notice of the biggest clusters. The biggest clusters are likely to indicate what an employee truly thinks or feels in comparison to what he is verbally saying.

- Reflect upon what you learned about your employee by clustering his nonverbal signals.

CREATE FLEXIBLE BASELINES

Anytime we collect data we create "reports"–at least informally in our brains. With all the nonverbal data you will be collecting in even just one conversation, you will end up creating a nonverbal baseline report.

Documenting your baseline data and conclusions is a great idea. In this way, you really get to know how an employee uses their nonverbal signals in their own unique way, and it improves your accuracy at understanding the employee.

Meanwhile, it is also important to acknowledge that having this baseline can be a double-edged sword if you do not keep the baseline flexible. People change, and you do not want to be using a rigid, set-in-cement baseline. Keep modifying the baseline itself, according to subsequent conversations with your employee.

EXERCISE 13: NONVERBAL BASELINES

As mentioned, the baseline is your "report," your conclusions based on the nonverbals signals, the translations, and the clusters. By putting all of this information together, you can create a basic profile of your employee.

The baseline will give you an idea of how the employee uses her nonverbal signals and the best translations for her nonverbal signals.

- Create the original baseline by noting:

    - The nonverbal signals that the employee uses often. Include your translations of the employee's nonverbal signals.

    - The situations in which the employee's verbal messages match her nonverbal signals.

    - The situations in which the employee's verbal messages don't match her nonverbal signals. For instance, an employee may have difficulty expressing disagreement and it is only through the nonverbal signals that you will be able to recognize this employee's truth.

- Going forward: After a conversation with an employee, reflect upon what you knew about her use of nonverbal signals by reviewing the baseline information you had.

- Does anything you learned in the latest conversation change the baseline? If so, in what ways?

- Note, with each conversation you have with an employee, the baseline can change. At the same time, baselines rarely change dramatically or quickly.

THREE:
PINPOINT THE NONVERBAL SIGNALS

You have gathered the data, translated the raw data into valuable information, organized the information into clusters, created a baseline understanding of the information—so it is now time to pinpoint. This is a process of highlighting the most significant information.

You are looking for the information that will most benefit your goal of connection. This is not about judging or evaluating the employee. Remember, Connect & Succeed is about getting to know your employee on a deeper level, and using this knowledge to better connect with him.

EXERCISE 14: PINPOINTING THE NONVERBALS

- Bring your attention to the current conversation and identify and translate the nonverbal signals while also clustering and baselining them.

- To help guide you in your pinpointing, you can look at your overall baseline understanding of this employee, and note the most significant clusters from your previous conversations.

- Pinpoint, or choose to focus on, the nonverbal signals that seem most important and pertinent to the current conversation. Use this information to make your energetic listening most effective and successful.

- A Tip: The most important part of pinpointing is to trust your decisions about what to pinpoint. And remembering that everything is fluid in a conversation, you can adjust your pinpointing as the conversation continues.

ENERGETIC LISTENING
SUMMARY

PAY ATTENTION

- Deal With Distractions
- Expand Your Attention Span
- Raise Your Connection Awareness

PINPOINT THE NONVERBALS

- Identify and Translate the Nonverbal Signals
- Use Clusters and Baselines
- Pinpoint the Nonverbal Signals

III.
TARGETED SPEAKING

CHAPTER FIVE

Speak With Clarity

As a manager, you will be sharing information, instructions, and more with your employees. Naturally, speaking with clarity comes from you knowing your information and being able to communicate it in a clear, coherent, and articulate way.

There is also much more depth to truly speaking with clarity and Targeted Speaking will take you there. So from this point forward, you will assume your ability to speak clearly as defined above. This then allows you to dive more deeply in, and see the enhancements of Targeted Speaking.

As a Connect & Succeed manager, you want to speak with a clarity that honors the person you are speaking to. Specifically this means that you focus on not just saying what you want to say, but on how to best communicate what you want to say to the unique employee you are interacting with. By speaking with clarity, you are showing that you care about the employee, because you are speaking in a way that both effectively communicates and connects.

If you have a large number of employees who report to you, this may seem like an overwhelming task, but in one-on-one conversations, once you learn and implement your Targeted Speaking skills, this approach to speaking will be a natural part of your Connect & Succeed style.

There are three major points to consider in speaking with clarity in a Targeted Speaking way:

1. You must learn to tailor your message to the specific employee you are speaking to.

2. You want to consider your speaking style, both verbally and nonverbally. How the message is delivered can have a huge impact on the success of not only the communication, but also the connection.

3. Finally, as you speak, you want to highlight the common ground to your employee. You do this by seeking mutual understanding, identifying the common ground, then, by speaking of it, you highlight it. Common ground gives a platform to clarity.

TAILOR YOUR MESSAGE

Your ability to tailor your message can have a huge impact on how your message is received and understood. You know what you are trying to communicate but if you only evaluate its clarity from your point of view, you could be way off.

SPECIFIC FACTORS IN TAILORING YOUR MESSAGE

Some of the specific factors to consider in the tailoring of your message:

BACKGROUND INFORMATION

Your employee is very likely to be hearing the information in your message for the first time. This might mean that you need to provide some background to the information. In the same way a story works best with a beginning, middle, and end, all kinds of information benefits from a "proper" introduction, middle, and conclusion. For instance, if you are telling your employees about a new policy prohibiting eating lunch at their desks, it might be very useful to introduce the issue with an overview of the problems caused by employees eating lunch at their desks. The extent of background information you provide would depend on how up-to-date a specific employee is on the topic.

PERSONALITY OF THE EMPLOYEE

Another factor may be the personality of that specific employee. For instance, some people may have a personality that needs to hear the "whole story," but others may not. Considering the employee's individual personality goes a long way in Targeted Speaking.

THE SPECIFIC SITUATION

The circumstances around a conversation topic will be different for different employees. For example, the employee who does not need the background information about the new lunch policy may meet a friend for lunch in the cafeteria every day and not have any desire to eat lunch at her desk. The employee who wants the background information may be someone who eats at his desk often. Maybe he is taking classes at night, and the lunch hour is also his study hour. He is going to need more information about a new policy that will affect him so directly.

ON-GOING MODIFICATION

This tailoring of your message is an ongoing process. You will check the employee's reactions and understanding as you speak, and modify your message accordingly. You do not want to over-communicate and leave the employee overwhelmed with information or instructions. On the other hand, you don't want an employee confused because of too little information. As the conversation proceeds, you are modifying the message towards the most clarity for that specific employee.

GUIDELINES FOR TAILORING YOUR MESSAGE

When tailoring your message, there are two guidelines to consider:

1. On a positive note, a simple conversational technique of

matching your vocabulary to each employee will help you to tailor your message in a very successful way.

2. On a more cautionary note, an easy way to derail a conversation is to offend the employee you are speaking with. You definitely want to stay away from any remarks that could be construed as sexist, racist, or homophobic.

MATCH VOCABULARIES

If you use a vocabulary that takes into account the experience, education, personal characteristics and sophistication of each employee, you will increase your ability to connect exponentially.

Although everyone usually shares a basic vocabulary there are also wide variations in the words used by different employees. Consider the following words:

- likely
- probable
- possible
- plausible
- conceivable

They all mean approximately the same thing, but are also slightly different. Your goal with targeted speaking is to use the best word, the word that most effectively communicates and connects you to the employee you are speaking with.

EXERCISE 15: MATCH VOCABULARIES

An important part of tailoring your message is to match your vocabulary to the employee you are in conversation with.

- Before meeting with an employee, reflect upon the employee, and considering what message you have to deliver, think about the words that would be most effective with this specific employee.

- During the conversation, notice if your words are hitting the right mark, and adjust your vocabulary as needed.

DO NOT OFFEND

Of course you do not want to make any comments that can be taken as sexist, racist, or homophobic. First and foremost, many such comments would violate Federal and State laws, as well as company policies. From a Connect & Succeed standpoint, they represent the complete opposite of what Connect & Succeed is about. Such comments are inappropriate and unproductive.

As a Connect & Succeed manager you must be aware of the language you can and cannot use in the workplace. This may seem an obvious point, but it is unfortunately, one that still needs to be said.

Also, while some language and comments are certainly inappropriate, there are not only some grey areas in language, but also differences in what people find offensive. For instance, if you call the people who work in your computer department "geeks," they could see it as a badge of honor or find it demeaning.

Since at a minimum, any offensive remarks will disrupt the workplace and interfere with productivity, you, as a Connect & Succeed manager, want to error on the side of caution in this area. The good news is that if you are using all the techniques and skills of the Connect & Succeed style, you will be paying attention to the employee, and be able to pick up on cues and clues that indicate any offense the employee might be feeling. This is good because in cases of offensive comments, severe harm can be done very quickly.

EXERCISE 16: DO NOT OFFEND

Use the following tips to help you stay on track with your Targeted Speaking.

- When speaking to an employee, stay alert to how the employee is receiving your message. If you detect any offense taken on the part of the employee, deal with it immediately. Remember, the strength of the Connect & Succeed style is the good relationships that you have with your employees.

- Keep track of the language your employees use with each other, but do not assume that if they use the language with each other, that it is automatically ok for you, as their manager, to use the same language.

- Avoid using language or making comments that are potentially offensive. This is not about walking on egg shells about what you say. This is about caring about and respecting your employees, and letting this show via your interactions with them.

CONSIDER YOUR SPEAKING STYLE

Your success as a targeted speaker is influenced by more than just what you say. Your speaking style speaks "loudly" to your ability to clearly communicate and connect.

There are several factors to consider as you speak. At first, thinking about these factors in the course of a conversation may feel awkward, but the more you create a style that feels true to you while also applying the principles of Connect & Succeed, the easier this will all be.

The factors that create your speaking style include:

- Volume
- Speaking speed
- Enunciation

Additionally, the following three skills can help you to successfully target your speaking:

- Speak in short increments
- Use congruent nonverbals
- Speak with honest emotion

SPEAK IN SHORT INCREMENTS

When you target your speaking, do so in shorter increments. Break up what you say into understandable bites. Make your comments succinct, and cover only one topic at a time. Long extended speeches covering multiple topics do not help the employee grasp what you are talking about. You overwhelm her with information.

When an employee is overwhelmed, she makes arbitrary decisions about what to process and what to ignore. What she chooses may not be the information you wanted to emphasize, but it is the best she can do in the given situation. Information overload will not help you to connect and succeed.

When you speak in shorter increments, you enable the employee to more effectively handle the information you are sharing. If an employee is unclear about anything you are saying, speaking in shorter increments gives him a chance to process what you are saying and/or formulate and ask questions. In fact, you will want to incorporate "pauses" into your targeted speaking in order to give your employee the chance to express agreement or disagreement, or to ask clarifying questions.

There are, of course, times when your topic is big and there is a lot to say. It is even more important to speak in short increments in this case. Take that big topic and divide it into smaller topics, so you can still incorporate the pauses into your targeted speaking. In the end, the clarity gained will be worthwhile.

EXERCISE 17: SHORT INCREMENTS

Two parts to this exercise: Practice the art of breaking down your topics into smaller pieces, and practice speaking in these smaller increments.

Learning to break down any topic into smaller pieces is valuable beyond the Connect & Succeed conversation. For instance, when writing or giving a speech.

• Take a given set of information and break it

down into sub-categories. This could be a policy at work or a decision to buy a new car. Take the overall information and break it down into its parts. Suggestion: Do this as a written exercise.

- As for practicing speaking in smaller increments, plan ahead. When you know you are going to have a Connect & Succeed conversation with an employee, take the information you need to share and break it down to its parts. This will give you a concise and logical way to present the information. Remember, the goal of your conversations with employees is not just to tell them something. The goal is also to connect and create a relationship.

USE CONGRUENT NONVERBALS

The second speaking style factor that can help you connect and succeed is the use of congruent nonverbals. In Chapter 4 we discussed the topic of nonverbal communication as it relates to Energetic Listening. You also want to understand the impact your nonverbal signals have on your ability to speak with clarity. If your nonverbals are not congruent with your message, clarity will jump out the window.

While the focus of this section is on keeping your nonverbal communication on the same wavelength as what you are saying, it should be noted that the very nature of the manager-employee relationship creates a situation where your employees are always, consciously or unconsciously, tuning into what you are saying in your nonverbal signals. They are continually reading even the most subtle signs from you.

For example, in one of my management positions I had to announce a new policy that would eliminate the cost-of-living raises for everyone in my department for three years. I did not like this policy, but I did not want to communicate this to my employees, for fear of squashing morale and decreasing my employees' engagement and motivation. I made the announcement in what I felt was a "neutral" way, without expressing my own thoughts and feelings. After the meeting however, I heard that it was clear to everyone that I did not like the new "no raise" decision. My nonverbal signals gave me away.

There are two ways to look at congruency in your nonverbal signals:

- When targeting your speaking, you want your non-verbal signals to match what you are saying.
- Studies show that when our nonverbals signals match those of the person we are talking to, they are more likely to connect with you. Therefore, as part of your Targeted Speaking style, you have a proven technique to connect with your employees as you are speaking to them.

Creating a congruency between your verbal and nonverbal messages is not so much a difficult task as it is an awareness.

Some of my coaching clients ask me which message is the "right" one, and we have found that sometimes there are two or more messages that are "right." Not everything is black and white. That said, you need to consciously decide what the message is that you want to deliver, what message feels the most "true," and match your verbal and nonverbal signals—otherwise, you will create confusion, and confusion is definitely not good for connecting and succeeding.

EXERCISE 18:
MATCH YOUR VERBAL & NONVERBAL SIGNALS

This exercise is about being observant and reflecting on this topic.

- As discussed earlier in this book, you have undoubtedly had many conversational experiences where the speaker was saying one thing, and you were getting a very different message via his nonverbal signals. How did it make you feel as the listener?

- You have also experienced situations where your own nonverbal signals told a different story than your words. What did you say and what nonverbal signals did not align with what you said? How did this feel?

- Also note the situations where you or another speaker's verbal and nonverbals messages were a match. Did it strengthen the verbal message? Was the message clearer to the listener? How did it feel?

MATCH YOUR NONVERBAL SIGNALS
WITH THE LISTENER'S NONVERBAL SIGNALS

The ability to connect with someone is increased by similarity.

Studies show that we like people with names similar to our own. The same goes with people who have birthdays near ours. Mimicking body and other nonverbal signals is also effective in getting people to like you. Taken further, many salespeople are trained to mimic the body language of the people they are talking to, as a method to increase their sales.

This awareness can help your Targeted Speaking. A big scale example of this is the camaraderie created when all the fans of an athletic team share the same gesture of support. On a smaller scale, think about the slight but significant head nod, and how your adding of a head nod to acknowledge the head nod of your listener will improve the impact of your speaking. Let's try it!

EXERCISE 19: MATCH NONVERBAL SIGNALS

Take a playful approach to this exercise and see what happens.

- In your conversation with an employee, observe and identify some of the nonverbal gestures she uses frequently.
- Use these same gestures at appropriate times as you speak.
- Note the difference this matching of nonverbal gestures makes in your ability to connect to this employee.

SPEAK WITH HONEST EMOTION

The third factor in your speaking style is to speak with honest emotion. Whether conscious of it or not, your employees will pick up on the emotions behind what you say as a manager. As with the nonverbal signals, the emotions that filter through are often more important than the actual content of what you say.

For example: My coaching client, Laurie, told a story about telling an employee that she had complete confidence in his leadership, as she handed a big project over to him. Unfortunately, this was not true, and this doubt seeped into the conversation. This meant that the employee received different messages from the conversation and was left feeling confused. This also meant the project got off to a rough start. Luckily, Laurie, as a Connect & Succeed manager, remedied the situation quite quickly by having a follow-up conversation where she shared her doubts with the employee. This cleared the air, and allowed for a much better connection between the two of them. In the end, the project was completed successfully. Working honestly at all levels is a winner.

As an Energetic Listener, you are asked to acknowledge the emotions behind what your employee is saying. Now you are also being asked to "tune into" your own emotions as you speak. Additionally, you can track the emotional impact you are having on the employee by tuning into the emotional contagion you are initiating. Let's dive into each of these:

TUNE INTO YOUR OWN EMOTIONS

Communication and connection always have an emotional component. Because your emotions have such a meaningful affect on your communication style, you want to develop your ability to understand your unique emotions on a deep level.

Getting in touch with your own emotions will strengthen your ability to connect with your employees. They will pick up on the emotional honesty behind your words, and that is a "frequency" that will add meaning to what you say. When you speak from such depth, you will truly speak with clarity.

If you use this tool unconsciously, it can cause problems, like saying one thing and feeling another. But used consciously, and for the purposes of connection, your emotions can be used in very positive ways, and can be a great asset in creating the connection you want from your targeted speaking.

EXERCISE 20: TUNE INTO YOUR EMOTIONS

Even with your enhanced awareness as a Connect & Succeed manager, your emotions will show up as you speak. Therefore, the more aware you are of them, the better.

- Write down a short synopsis of a given topic. Follow this by a list of emotions you feel around this topic. Notice that you always have emotions around any given topic.
- Specifically, before a planned Connect & Succeed conversation, make the list of emotions as described above. Knowing this before going into a conversation will be useful.

TAKE ADVANTAGE OF EMOTIONAL CONTAGION

You have already been introduced to emotional contagion in Chapter 3. It is both an Energetic Listening and a Targeted Speaking skill. In review, it refers to the way people will pick up on the emotions another person brings into the room. It is something that, for the most part, happens naturally and unconsciously. The great news is that as a Connect & Succeed manager, you can again use emotional contagion for good!

Remembering that your goal is to connect with your employee, think about how much more powerful this connection can be if you come to it with a emotion that you want to share. If you come to the conversation with enthusiasm, or excitement, or gratitude and you can "spread" this feeling to your employee, connection will be easier to achieve. For one thing, you will have the common ground of this shared emotion on which to build more connection. This is another win-win situation.

EXERCISE 21: USE EMOTIONAL CONTAGION

- When you tune into your emotions, you become aware of the emotions you have around a given topic. As a manager going into a conversation with an employee, you can then choose the emotions that you want to inform your side of the conversation.

- As you choose this emotion, be aware of emotional contagion. For instance, if you want your employee to be open to an idea, bring an emotion that will invite openness.

- As you target your speaking, let the chosen emotion inform your speaking.

- Note: This is not about manipulating the employee. Remember, the goal of the Connect & Succeed conversation is about connection – honest, long-term connection.

HIGHLIGHT THE COMMON GROUND

The last major point of speaking with clarity is to highlight the common ground as you speak. The more common ground, the more clarity. The more clarity in your targeted speaking, the greater the chance of connection. By shining the light on your shared interests, you improve the conversation itself, and deepen the connection you have with your employee. This is what Connect & Succeed is all about.

In order to highlight common ground as you speak, you take the following steps:

- Seek mutual understanding
- Identify the common ground
- Speak of the common ground to your employee

SEEK MUTUAL UNDERSTANDING

It can't be emphasized enough that targeted speaking is so much more than saying what you want to say. It is that plus the mutual understanding that is developed from what you say. This seemingly puts the goal markers further out, but in reality, it just offers a goal that is more fruitful.

When you use your Targeted Speaking to seek mutual under-standing with your employee, you will be laying the groundwork for common ground.

Note that mutual understanding and agreement are not the same. At best, there is an overlap between the two, but you do not have to be in agreement to share some mutual understanding of a given issue or topic. For instance, you and the employee may share an understanding about the ultimate outcome of a project, and you both understand that a particular portion of the project will take the most time, but you disagree on how much time and how many employees it will take. In discussing this issue, you want to use your mutual understanding as a foundation from which to discuss the other factors.

Mutual understanding may require some extra steps in your conversation. Specifically, you will seek honest input and feedback from the employee you are speaking with, and fill in and clarify places where there is no mutual understanding.

ASK FOR FEEDBACK

Because understanding cannot be a one-sided activity, you, as the manager, must actively seek the feedback of your employee. In this Targeted Speaking chapter, we are recognizing that you need to do this not only when listening energetically to the employee; you need to do this when taking your speaking turn in the conversation.

Furthermore, the more successful you are in eliciting open and honest feedback and input from your employee, the stronger the mutual understanding that can be developed. Obviously, the observations you make as an energetic listener are the first steps to mutual understanding. Now, as a targeted speaker, you can both formally and informally ask and invite input from the employee.

Not every manager feels comfortable asking for feedback from employees. Some managers feel that they should have all the answers. Asking for employee feedback is not admitting a weakness. When you admit that you do not know everything and need employee input you are perceived by employees as more human. Employees are better able to relate to someone who is open to feedback.

PAUSE AND ASK

Informally, during the conversation and as you are speaking, take a pause and ask "What do you think of this idea?" or "What are your ideas on completing our new project on time and within budget?" You could address the issue of mutual understanding more directly and say: "I want to be sure I am being clear on this. What questions or concerns do you have?" A more formal ask would be a request for a specific meeting to discuss the employee's feedback on how a particular project is progressing. Also note that the more open-ended the question, the larger the chance of developing mutual understanding. Yes or no questions tend to limit conversations.

More important than the method of asking for feedback is simply the fact that you asked for it. Remember, when employees feel cared about, the motivation and engagement goes up. As a Connect & Succeed manger, you want to automatically think of your employees as full contributors on every project.

ALLOW HONESTY

Also, the best mutual understanding comes from honesty. Employees should not be afraid of any negative repercussions when they offer feedback. Do not get defensive if you do not agree with the feedback they are providing. Remember, you asked for the feedback in the first place.

FILL IN AND CLARIFY

Because you are seeking mutual understanding, and because you asked for feedback, you will want to fill in and clarify your information according to your employee's feedback.

This is where conversation can go off track. Don't put yourself into a defensive mode. Understand that communication is a complex endeavor, and while you believe you have been clear, what this employee heard was not the same as what you thought you said. Remember that Targeted Speaking is all about caring about the employee, and that wonderful success goal of connection.

EXERCISE 22: MUTUAL UNDERSTANDING

- As you speak, stay tuned into your employee's understanding of what you are saying.

- Ask for the employee's feedback with open-ended questions and comments.

    Have some open-ended questions and comments ready to go. Prepare these questions and comments ahead of time and make them part of your Connect & Succeed style.

    Create questions that add encouragement instead of "contest." For example, instead of "Do you agree with me?" you could say, "I would love to hear your feedback on this idea. What do you think?"

- According to the feedback, fill in and clarify what you are saying.

- Remember that you are seeking mutual understanding and that even when there is disagreement, there is also some mutual understanding.

IDENTIFY THE COMMON GROUND

If you and your employee have sought and found a mutual understanding, you can move to the next step of identifying your common ground. At this point, your willingness to find common ground in all types of circumstances and your openness to common ground in general are factors in just how much common ground you will be able to discover.

A reminder from Chapter 2 about the kind of common ground you are looking for: Connect & Succeed common ground is the place where something about you – your ideas, stories, personality, interests, viewpoints, backgrounds, preferences, idiosyncrasies, etc. – intersects and overlaps with something about the person you are talking to.

Once you recognize your common ground, you can highlight it to your employee as you target your speaking. Working from places of common ground will give you points of clarity with your employee.

Take the example of talking with one of your employees about a project that she is leading. In the course of the conversation you realize that both of you have led similar projects in the past. Yes! You have found common ground.

In the next section, we will discuss your Connect & Succeed connection and how common ground is a key component, but for now, we will look at common ground as a specific way to target your speaking. This means we are focused on the common ground you can find as you are speaking.

SPEAK OF THE COMMON GROUND

In the previous example, you realized that you and the employee had lead similar projects in the past. The Connect & Succeed strategy would be to now highlight that shared experience and talk openly about it. You then can explore lessons learned as you build a common ground based on those similar projects.

Generally, once you identify the common ground you share with the employee, you target your speaking through the common ground, thus making what you say more palatable and inviting to that specific employee. By highlighting the common ground, you add clarity to your connection.

EXERCISE 23:
IDENTIFY AND SPEAK OF COMMON GROUND

Identify Common Ground

- While you are speaking, run your radar for points of common ground.

  - Tip: Look for points of common ground related to the work environment, and also outside of it. Don't be afraid to take a small tangent to discuss how you both hate the recent weather. It might lead to some deeper common ground.

Speak of the Common Ground

- Take the initiative to use your Targeted Speaking to point out the common ground you share with the employee.

CHAPTER SIX

Support The Speaker

Chapter 5 looked at how to enhance your conversations with Targeted Speaking. In this chapter, you will see how Targeted Speaking is used to encourage and support the employee to take an active role in the conversation. This is particularly important in the manager-employee relationship, where the company's managerial structure may discourage an employee from speaking up when in conversation with a manager.

This is a also a perfect illustration of how speaking and listening intertwine in actual conversations. In the Connect & Succeed style, this aspect of Targeted Speaking overlaps with Energetic Listening, and highlights the complex wonders of even the simplest of conversations. In fact, this aspect of your Targeted Speaking will be used during the parts of the conversation where you are "officially" a listener.

The goal of this Targeted Speaking is also focused on making the employee feel cared about. In other words, heard, respected, and valued. As a Targeted Speaker, you can support the speaker, your employee, in any conversation. The real key to this support is not just that you are listening, but that the speaker knows you are listening and caring. It is also important that this support continues throughout the conversation.

The more you can actively acknowledge the speaker, the better. This acknowledgement supports and encourages the employee to speak up, to speak honestly and openly, and to feel like a valued member of your department. You can acknowledge the employee verbally or nonverbally.

In Chapter 5, you learned to identify and highlight points of common ground as a way to achieve more clarity in your conversations by speaking of the common ground. In this chapter, you will approach the spotlighting of common ground from the other side of the conversation—as a listener who develops common ground with the speaker through your responses to what the employee says. You will speak to the common ground. It is all good!

Finally, you will learn to deal with disagreement in a Targeted Speaking way. At this point, you can't let a little disagreement get in the way of your connection... or your success. But there will be disagreements, and so there is a Connect & Succeed approach to them.

Let's now look more deeply into the three Connect & Succeed "tools" you can use to support the speaker:

- Actively Acknowledge the Speaker
- Spotlight the Common Ground
- Deal with Disagreement

ACTIVELY ACKNOWLEDGE THE SPEAKER

When you actively acknowledge the speaker, whether verbally or nonverbally, you show interest in what he is saying. You support and encourage the speaker. You invite him to continue to speak. All of this makes the speaker, your employee, feel engaged and motivated. Win-win-win.

VERBAL ACKNOWLEDGMENTS

There are several ways to verbally acknowledge and support the speaker during a conversation. These include the use of

- Audio flow comments
- Paraphrasing
- Questions and supportive comments

USE AUDIO FLOW COMMENTS

Audio flow comments are simple, small comments such as "Yes," or "Uh huh." They can be a huge booster to the speaker. Small comments are perfect in this situation because they affirm the speaker, but do not interrupt the speaker's flow.

EXERCISE 24: AUDIO FLOW COMMENTS

- Notice how well you verbalize your audio flow comments. Do you interrupt the flow? Do you forget to say them out loud?

- Notice what audio flow comments you normally use during a conversation. Experiment with some that might be even more proactive in their support and encouragement, and see if it makes a difference for your employees.

PARAPHRASE

By simply repeating what a person has said, you go a long way in supporting that person. When you paraphrase, and "repeat" the message in your own words, you show the speaker that you are paying attention and truly engaging on a deep level. You are meeting at the meaning level.

Paraphrasing is an acknowledgment of the speaker and leads to connection with that person. It is human nature to appreciate acknowledgment.

EXERCISE 25: PARAPHRASING

- Practice paraphrasing with either written or spoken material. You can practice paraphrasing individual statements or sentences, or longer material where you will be combining the paraphrasing with summarizing.

- During the conversation, make sure to share your paraphrase with the employee as a way of indicating your interest in what he is saying.

- Notice and note the reactions from your employees when you practice this acknowledgement during the conversation. Notice how it can open up connection.

ASK RELEVANT QUESTIONS AND MAKE SUPPORTIVE COMMENTS

In the last chapter, we had you asking questions and making comments to elicit feedback. In this chapter on supporting the speaker, the questions and comments have a different goal: They are questions meant to acknowledge and support the speaker.

For example, instead of asking, "What do you think about this idea I just presented?" you would be asking a question about what the speaker just said: "Where did you come up with this great idea?" or "How soon do you think you could implement such an action?" Even questions and comments that are not as "complimentary" can feel supportive: "I love the way this is going, but I am wondering about how many people would be needed for such a project."

As a Connect & Succeed manager you want to use these questions and comments to prompt the speaker to say more. You might have seen some managers use their questions and/or comments as a way to cut off or interrogate their employees. That is not your goal.

The questions themselves should not be just "yes or no" questions. Make your questions open-ended to encourage your employee to continue to speak, and likely at a deeper and more authentic level. Comments can sometimes be thought of as "end points," so make sure the comments invite the employee to respond. Sometimes, comments and questions can be combined: "You are making me worry about our deadline, so can you tell me more about the timetable you are thinking about?"

As for the relevance of your questions, it is, of course, key to ask questions that relate to what the person has just said. If you ask a question out of left field, the employee can easily jump to the conclusion that you are not really listening to her. If you ask a question that relates to something your employee said earlier, remember to mention that the reference is from an earlier part of the conversation.

EXERCISE 26:
QUESTIONS & COMMENTS

Practice the creation of relevant questions and supportive comments by using written or spoken material to create them. Suggestions: Use written news articles, reports, or even stories. Listen to podcasts, news programming, films or television.

- As you read or listen, write down the questions and/or comments that come to you.
- Review the list for the questions and comments that are both useful to you and would be supportive to the speaker.
- Highlight those questions and comments
- During your conversation with an employee, use your practiced skill of coming up with relevant questions and supportive comments. Notice which ones work and which ones do not.

- After the conversation, reflect upon other questions or comments that might have worked.

NONVERBAL ACKNOWLEDGMENTS

We have covered the pinpointing of nonverbal signals when listening, as well as the matching of nonverbal signals as you seek clarity in your speaking. Now we want to look at how you can use nonverbal signals to acknowledge and support the speaker, and further, to encourage and invite the speaker to continue speaking.

Let's look specifically at a few of the nonverbal signals that can be used to support your speaker:

- Eye contact
- Supportive gestures
- Personal space and touch

MAKE AND MAINTAIN EYE CONTACT

Keeping eye contact with your employee as he speaks is crucial to a good Connect & Succeed conversation. After all, if you are looking at him, it is a strong indication that you are listening. Eye contact is both this simple, and at the same time, a complex feature of nonverbal communication.

The eyes can be the most expressive nonverbal feature. They can indicate a positive or negative mood. Eye contact can indicate interest, attention, and involvement or inattention and boredom. They can express emotions of happiness or attraction, or sadness or anger. They can encourage or intimidate. Eye movements can include looking up, down, or sideways, gazing, glancing, staring, squinting, blinking, winking, closing, and other combinations of these movements.

Adding to this complexity is the fact that there are distinct individual differences in both the eye contact you give, and how the employee will interpret your eye contact. So stay aware, and if your eye contact seems to make your employee uncomfortable at all, lighten up. Also remember that the next employee you speak with might just welcome the same level of eye contact that made the first person uncomfortable.

Indeed, the fact is that at every corner of communication and connection, the one-on-one conversation is ripe with potential, and yet, each conversation is unique, and therefore no hard and fast rules can be set in stone. Of course, this is what makes it all, especially your Connect & Succeed style, so exciting and dynamic.

A final note on eye contact, that actually applies to all nonverbal acknowledgments, is that you can reveal more than you plan on revealing. For instance, you could be tired at work that day because of a plumbing problem at your house the night before. This distraction could leak through when your eye contact wanders during a conversation with an employee. The employee could then assume that you are not interested in what she is saying.

OFFER SUPPORTIVE GESTURES

Supportive gestures, such as a slight nod or tilt of the head, are very effective ways to support the speaker. Equally potent is a simple smile. It is difficult to continue speaking to a scrowling face. On the other hand, a smiling face is an invitation.

Another nonverbal factor is your posture. The more positive and open it is, the more supported your employee will feel. Small adjustments can make a huge difference. For instance, a slight lean in is generally more supportive than a lean out. There can be a mere matter of degrees between the lean in and the lean out, but the lean in will make the speaker feel supported and the lean out makes the speaker think you want to leave the conversation. These positions may not even be conscious—but they will have an impact.

Some people have a tendency to cross their arms in front of their bodies while listening to a speaker. You can see how this pose could easily make the speaker feel like you are not open to what he has to say. It can feel like a defensive posture to the speaker and will shut down connection.

Here is yet another perfect spot to mention the complexity of communication, and specifically the need to stay aware of what your nonverbal signals are signaling to the other person. If you are crossing your arms in front of your body for any reason, you need to remain aware of the general tendency to translate crossed arms as a defensive signal. Therefore, it might behoove you to mention why you are making this gesture, and separate it from the communication between you and your employee.

SUPPORT WITH PERSONAL SPACE & TOUCH

There are some nonverbal signals that can get very mixed reviews. On one hand, they can be highly effective at supporting the speaker. On the other hand, they can be seen as violations by some employees. As mentioned before, Connect & Succeed understands that in communication it is more than what you intend with your words or actions; it is also how the other person, in this case, your employee, interprets and perceives your words and actions. Both personal space and touch are nonverbal factors that can support your employee, but you must stay aware of how your gestures are being perceived. You do not want to make any of your employees uncomfortable.

PERSONAL SPACE

Personal space is an area that people establish around themselves. It is an invisible boundary that people create, usually subconsciously, over time. This is their comfort zone, and they usually don't want just anyone intruding within that space. Also, this space is unique to each person and the dimensions can range from inches to feet.

Failing to respect the personal space of an employee can provoke extreme emotional and physical reactions. These reactions can, of course, be an obstacle to connection with that employee.

As a Connect & Succeed manager, you identify and keep track of the personal space preferences of every one of your employees. For example, which of your employees can you stand close to when talking? Which of your employees require "a little more space"? You learn your employees' personal space preferences by interacting with them and remembering what you have discovered from one conversation to the next. The personal space preferences of an employee do not change much once established, but it is a good idea to use your energetic listening and targeted speaking to continue to verify your employees' boundaries in each conversation.

TOUCH

As with personal space, people vary widely in the type and amount of touch they feel comfortable with. As a Connect & Succeed manager you will find the appropriate level of touch with each of your employees. Because Energetic Listening and Targeted Speaking are focused on you truly caring about and interacting with your employees, this will be easier than you think. Really in all areas of communication, but particularly in this area, be willing to err on the side of comfort. In other words, if you don't know that an employee would be comfortable with a touch of support on the shoulder, then don't do it. Find another way, verbally or nonverbally, to support this speaker.

Even with the so-called "safe" gestures, such as a hand shake, high five, or pat on the back, you will want to stay tuned in to how your employee is perceiving your gesture. Remember, the goal here is to make the speaker feel cared about, and you have lots of tools in your Connect and Succeed toolbox to accomplish this goal.

EXERCISE 27: NONVERBAL ACKNOWLEDGMENTS

Nonverbal Acknowledgments are important and the more aware you stay about what messages you are sending, the stronger your Targeted Speaking.

Approach the following exercises with curiosity and find what works for you and your employees. It is good to try new nonverbal techniques, but stay in your own comfort zone, because your employees will pick up on your discomfort if you are pushing things too far.

- **Eye Contact**
  - Be aware of both your eye contact, and how comfortable you feel about making the contact. Additionally, be aware of how each employee responds to your eye contact.
  - Note that just because someone seems to feel uncomfortable with your normal level of eye contact, it does not automatically mean that that person is uncomfortable with you.

- **Supportive Gestures and Cues**
  - Experiment with your body language and observe how your employees respond. For instance: When speaking to one of your employees, notice the impact of an encouraging head nod.

- **Personal Space**
  - Get a sense of the circumference of your personal space. For all kinds of reasons, you have each developed, probably subconsciously, a circle of personal space that you feel comfortable with.
  - As you speak with your employees, notice the personal space requirements of each

one of them. Take note. Personal space is so important that once learned, you really want to respect it.

- In each conversation with each employee, keep his or her personal space in mind.

- **Touch**

  - In an approach similar to the personal space factor, start with yourself. Assess what types of touch you feel comfortable with.

  - As you speak with employees, notice what levels and types of touch they are comfortable with. This is a particularly important factor to get right.

  - In each conversation with each employee, keep her "touch parameters" front and center in your connection work. These are boundaries you do not cross.

COMBINING VERBAL AND NONVERBAL SUPPORT

Remember that none of the acknowledgment techniques have to be isolated actions. For instance, as you say "I see" you might lean in a bit. In terms of supporting your speaker, this is a two-pointer!

SPOTLIGHT THE COMMON GROUND

As mentioned earlier in this chapter, you **highlighted** the common ground to your employee as you spoke. Now, in this aspect of Targeted Speaking, you again find the common ground between you and your employee, and from this angle, **spotlight** it as a way to encourage your employee to continue the conversation and feel heard, respected, and valued.

One key factor that will help you identify the common ground you share with your employee is to activate your empathy. This will increase your ability to tune into the common ground. Once tuned in, it is a simple matter of using your Targeted Speaking to let your employee know that you acknowledge and honor this common ground. Let's face it, when you feel like you are on the same team with someone, you feel good.

ACTIVATE YOUR EMPATHY

Empathy is defined as the ability to identify with the feelings, thoughts, and attitudes of another. When you make the decision to tune into your empathy you show a sincere interest in understanding the other person and a curiosity about what they have experienced. You essentially acknowledge both the experiences of your employees, and how they feel about those experiences.

Empathy is a natural human ability, but its value can easily be ignored. With Connect & Succeed, on the other hand, since success is about how much connection can be established between you and each employee, you can easily see how being empathetic with an employee will be an ace in the hole. Being able to "walk in another person's shoes," even in your mind, opens you up in important ways.

IDENTIFY THE COMMON GROUND

Your activated empathy will help you identify the common ground in what your employee is saying. When you can empathize with a person, you will truly know where your common ground with him is, and through that common ground, you will know how to best support him.

Remember, the common ground you want to identify and speak to at this point is the common ground that will empower the speaker to continue to talk, keeping the connection active and vibrant. For instance, in the course of her speaking, your employee might mention how she once worked in a completely different wing of the company, doing something very different from what she does now. The difficulty of such a transition late in her career might then be a topic broached. This might be similar to your career trajectory at this company, and you can very much empathize with that type of transition and all the "character" it developed in you. Identifying this as common ground would be a good move towards supporting the employee.

SPEAK TO THE COMMON GROUND

At this point, you will be able to direct your Targeted Speaking to the common ground you find, and add invitation and inspiration to your support. For example, when you find out you had a career trajectory similar to your employee's, you can target this information and let the employee know that you share a similar experience. Of course, do this in a succinct way, so that you don't veer off into your experience. Focus on using this common ground to encourage the employee to share more about her experience.

When you put the spotlight on the common ground, your employee will feel the support and be motivated and engaged in your connection with her. This is the good stuff that leads to success.

EXERCISE 28: SPOTLIGHT THE COMMON GROUND

- **Activate Your Empathy**

  - Practice your ability to empathize: While others around you talk about other people by judging them, you can wonder what it would be like to be in their shoes.

  - You can be willing to look at the world from other points of view. "What if?" becomes an interesting question to you: What if that happened to me? What if I knew what that person knows? What if...?

  - Before your conversation with an employee even begins, consider what you know about this employee, and imagine the upcoming conversation from his point of view. What are his concerns and questions? What is he feeling? What does he hope for from this conversation with you?

- **Identify the Common Ground**
  - During the conversation, be aware of places you can identify as common ground. It is very likely that your employee will be telling you something without knowing you share an understanding, similar thought, etc. about it.
  - To help you find common ground, remember to use your activated empathy to open up the search.

- **Speak to the Common Ground**
  - During the conversation: Once you have identified some common ground, speak to it. This should then encourage your employee to feel heard and say more.
  - Further reflection after the conversation may also yield more common ground, especially if you review how the conversation went from your employee's "shoes."

DEAL WITH DISAGREEMENT

As mentioned at the beginning of this chapter, there will be disagreements. There are so many different perspectives and unique personalities that there will always be those situations where you and your employee will not agree and connection is difficult to create. Pretending there will not be disagreement would be naive. Instead, you will want to have a Connect & Succeed strategy for handling disagreements.

More than any other factor, disagreements interfere with productivity because they break down effective communication and connection between you and your employees. Identifying and dealing with disagreements thus becomes a key factor in achieving managerial success.

The first factor in dealing with disagreement is to recognize it as soon as possible. If your energetic listening picks up on any signs of disagreement, acknowledge it and deal with it. If you fail to do this, you run the risk of disagreement and conflicts simmering below the surface only to potentially blow up later. In addition, if you are obliviousness to the signs of disagreement, your targeted speaking will be based on false premises.

First off, you need to recognize that disagreeing with someone is not only an inevitable situation, but it is also not necessarily a bad thing. Sometimes the best ideas come when people differ in their approach. In fact, some of the best ideas come from situations that originally seemed irresolvable. Yet, disagreement still needs to be actively dealt with.

As a Connect & Succeed manager you will prepare for the disagreements that will inevitably occur. Furthermore, you can't be afraid to share your disagreement with employees. This is actually where Connect & Succeed shines, because if you can disagree with someone while continuing to listen to her, while still acknowledging the places where you share common ground, and that employee continues to feel cared about, the connection can be saved.

In this situation, your Targeted Speaking will actively acknowledge and discuss any disagreement while continuing to support the employee. This may seem to be quite a juggling act, but remember that as a Connect & Succeed manager, you are grounded in common ground connection, and when your employees know that you focus on and care about them, disagreements can be easier to resolve. The Connect & Succeed approach allows your employee to feel like she can fully express herself, which is often the thing that people most want, while you both can be honest about your disagreement.

This approach to disagreement between you and each employee will set the tone for your whole department. This Connect and Succeed strategy will create an atmosphere of open problem solving in which everyone is heard and respected.

Note: The Connect & Succeed communication style can also be very useful in helping to resolve employee-employee disagreements in your department.

EXERCISE 29: DEAL WITH DISAGREEMENT

Disagreements happen... and the first one in any type of relationship can be the toughest. So plan ahead and imagine that first disagreement with a given employee. This will give you a ready-to-go strategy and script, if or when it actually happens.

• Write out scenarios where you find yourself in disagreements with various employees you already have a Connect & Succeed relationship with. Consider all the "tools" from Energetic

Listening and Targeted Speaking that you can use to both honestly discuss the disagreement while keeping the connection viable. List these "tools."

• Also, write out Targeted Speaking scripts of what you might say to these employees as you create the outcome described above.

TARGETED SPEAKING
SUMMARY

SPEAK WITH CLARITY

- Tailor Your Message
- Consider Your Speaking Style
- Highlight The Common Ground

SUPPORT THE SPEAKER

- Actively Acknowledge the Speaker
- Spotlight The Common Ground
- Deal with Disagreement

IV.
COMMON GROUND
CONNECTION

CHAPTER SEVEN

Connect Through Common Ground

In the process of Energetic Listening and Targeted Speaking, you have already connected with your employee, because the whole Connect & Succeed conversation is about connecting. At the same time, in breaking down this part of the interaction, you can learn and further enhance your connection abilities.

Connect & Succeed is specifically focused on the common ground connection. Interestingly, if you think about it, almost all connection is based on some common ground. It is also the type of connection that is going to resonate most deeply between two people. Therefore, as a Connect & Succeed manager, your goal is connection via common ground.

This chapter is set up in three sections:

- Your Connect & Succeed Mindset
- Connection Through Common Ground
- Advanced Connection

First, there is a section on your Connect & Succeed Mindset. This is an important pre-step to your connection process. If you frame your mindset around common ground, connection will naturally follow.

Next is Common Ground Connection itself. Essentially you focus on and care about your employee, recognize the common ground, and reach out for connection. You can see how Energetic Listening and Targeted Speaking are essentially taking care of the first steps of Common Ground connection. You then want to make sure you follow through all the way to connection.

In the final section of this chapter, you will learn about two advanced connection factors that you can use to truly uplevel your Connect and Succeed style. These are advanced enhancers.

FRAME YOUR CONNECT & SUCCEED MINDSET

An important factor in being able to create connection with someone is your mindset. The more open you are to a Connect & Succeed connection, the more willing you are maximize your use of Energetic Listening and Targeted Speaking, and the more willing you are to let common ground upgrade your Connect & Succeed mindset.

There are five mindset keys for Common Ground Connection. You need to be open and willing, and accept other points of view. You also need to look out for your employees and truly enjoy connection. These five keys open up the door to a common ground connection mindset.

BE OPEN

In order to find common ground with an employee, it is necessary to be open on several fronts:

- You want to be open to the idea that you can always find common ground with each and every employee who reports to you. With some employees, and for whatever reasons, it will be more difficult to find the common ground, but it is always there – if you believe it is.

- You want to be open to the ideas, feelings, stories, and points of view of others, even if they are different from yours.

- You want to open to the idea that you can disagree with someone, and still find common ground on that very topic.

- You want to be open to all kinds of people, with all of their unique and idiosyncratic ways.

- You want to be open to yourself and therefore about yourself. Connection is best made when both sides are "invested."

BE WILLING

For a common ground mindset to take hold, you must be

willing to create the situations where common ground can be uncovered and connection can be made.

- As discussed in Chapter One, you must be willing to put some time and effort into becoming a Connect & Succeed style manager. But if you have been working the exercises in this book, you already know that the effort is well worth it, and the ROI (return on investment) is high.

- With Connect & Succeed, the one-on-one conversation is the "container" in which this connection is made. You must be willing to be proactive in making every conversation with an employee, a chance to connect or deepen an existing connection.

- You must be willing to start with only one point of common ground, and use the leverage to open the door wider as your relationship moves forward. In other words, you must be willing to step in even when the door is only open to a crack.

VALIDATE OTHER IDEAS AND POINTS OF VIEW

At this step, you need to not just be open to different ideas, feelings, stories and points of view, but also truly accept them, whether or not you agree with them.

Furthermore, you want to be open to the possibility that even though you are the manager, one of your employees could have a better idea about how to do something. Human nature makes some of us compete when hearing new ideas from others. Would you be able to accept and incorporate your employee's "better" idea, and give him full credit for it?

The very structure of most companies makes it difficult for a manager to validate other ideas and points of view. In fact, many managers feel a pressure to be the ones with the best ideas and points of view. If instead, you are willing to accept and validate the ideas, feelings, stories, and points of view of your employees, your path to Connect & Succeed success can be a super highway instead of a bumpy road.

LOOK OUT FOR YOUR EMPLOYEES

The research shows that when employees feel looked out for, their motivation and engagement at work goes up dramatically. If you want to be a dinosaur and cling to the out-dated managerial styles of top-down, "my way or the highway," "you work for me" thinking," Connect & Succeed is not for you. With every step, Connect & Succeed embraces the idea that looking out for your employees is the best and fastest way to success.

ENJOY CONNECTION

If you are a basketball player and you only care about winning, but don't get a thrill from the swosh of the ball hitting the net, you might consider another sport or activity that can give you the thrill of winning plus that basic and foundational level of enjoyment and satisfaction. In this same way, if you do not derive pleasure from making points of connection, big and small, Connect & Succeed might not be for you.

On the other hand, you would be highly advised to try it. On a very deep and human level, you are meant to connect. When you can tap into that, you will benefit yourself in multiple and large ways. The Connect & Succeed mindset alone will bring great gifts.

EXERCISE 30: MINDSET

Use each mindset factor as a prompt, and write down your thoughts and feelings around each concept. Note how each factor can help you connect with your employees.

- Be Open
- Be Willing
- Validate Other Ideas and Points of View
- Look Out for Your Employees
- Enjoy Connection
- Visualize your Connect & Succeed conversations with this mindset.
- Bring this mindset to all of your Connect & Succeed conversations.

CONNECT THROUGH COMMON GROUND

As mentioned at the beginning of this chapter, if you are using your Energetic Listening and Targeted Speaking, you are already connecting. Your Energetic Listening, Targeted Speaking, and Common Ground Connection are already intertwining and intersecting, so breaking them down into steps has been both silly and useful.

Furthermore, breaking down connection is a bit like trying to break down a kiss or driving a car. Of course, if you think back, there was probably a driver's education class in high school that broke down driving, and even just starting the car and pulling out of the parking space, into steps. And so with connection: There are steps, and they are presented, while also knowing that it is a fluid, sometimes indefinable, process. Yet armed with this information, you will find that your natural desire and ability to connect will rise to new levels.

The steps of Common Ground Connection are to:

- Focus On and Care About the Employee
- Use Common Ground
- Reach Out and Connect

Let's look at each step more closely:

FOCUS ON AND CARE ABOUT THE EMPLOYEE

You have seen these "mantras" throughout the previous chapters, particularly as key foundations for Energetic Listening and Targeted Speaking. The reason they are here again is because they are important. Think about it – when someone focuses his attention on you, you are much more likely to assume that there is common ground you share with this person, and that there is connection potential. When someone cares about you, you assume that you are a vital and important part of the team, and feeling heard, respected, and valued opens you up to connection.

This is a natural first step of connection, and a natural outcome of Energetic Listening and Targeted Speaking. It points you in the right direction and will increase your potential for success.

USE COMMON GROUND

In your Energetic Listening you gathered great material for common ground. You listened in a conscious, open-minded, and deep way, so it is highly likely that you found some common ground with your employee. And as part of your Targeted Speaking you identified and highlighted common ground in terms of what you brought to the conversation, and you spotlighted common ground from your employee.

REACH OUT AND CONNECT

In this last "step" you bring it all together, knowing that you can use any common ground you have uncovered to create connection. You "use" it first by just being aware of the common ground, then reaching out for connection in a way that matches it.

Or you might share common ground more proactively. Formally, it might be your decision to put a particular employee in charge of a specific part of your project. You would want to let her know that you know she would be great in this position because you share common ground with her. For example, you share a dedication to high quality work or like to work in collaboration. This is good for everyone.

Informally, the connection could be as simple as a quick coffee room discussion of a movie you know she saw over the weekend. All of this creates the kind of common ground connection that Connect & Succeed is about. So imagine these two examples... and a multitude of common ground possibilities in-between.

The important point is that you reach out for connection. In the end, all of the individual details and overall effect of a one-on-one conversation between you, the manager, and an employee, sets the stage for powerful and successful connection, which as you know from Chapter 1, reaps great rewards for you, your employee, and your company. Win-win-win!

EXERCISE 31:
CONNECT THROUGH COMMON GROUND

• Focus On and Care About the Employee

Assuming that you have been taking the steps needed to be a Connect & Succeed manager, you have focusing on and caring about your employees down! It is a step as reminder about the principles that reside at the center of Connect & Succeed.

• Use Common Ground

Although, it is not really secret, common ground is the "secret sauce" that brings the success. Remember, that with your Connect & Succeed skills, you can find common ground with almost anyone.

• **Reach Out and Connect**

You can do everything else involved with Connect & Succeed, but if you don't follow through and truly reach out and make the connection, you will not enjoy the view from the top of the mountain. Go for it!

ADVANCED CONNECTION

Connect & Succeed is all about enhancing your current connection ability, and even though the basic style as described so far will take you to the top of the mountain, there is more. There are two advanced communication elements that are great to know as you raise your levels of connecting and succeeding!

These advanced connection elements are:

- Thought Speed Gap
- Fully Formed Perspectives

THOUGHT SPEED GAP

The Thought Speed Gap is the difference between your speed of processing a conversation and the other person's speed of talking. It can be a huge asset to you in your Connect & Succeed conversations.

UNDERSTAND YOUR THOUGHT SPEED GAP

Most people talk at a rate of about 125-150 words per minute. As an energetic listener you can process information at least twice that fast, and theoretically up to 400-500 words per minute. This gives you "extra time" to process what the speaker is saying while still having your own thoughts and targeting your speaking. Admittedly, we are talking about fractions of a second, but those fractions add up in the life of a conversation. You can use this to your advantage.

You have actually used the Thought Speed Gap without realizing it. Here is an example one of my seminar participants, Samuel, shared: One of his employees came into the office dressed in baggy jeans and a tank top on "Casual Friday." It was definitely in violation of the company's dress code. Samuel needed to deal with this immediately, and asked the employee into his office for a conversation. This meant that Samuel did not have the time to really think about how he would handle the dress code violation, but while the employee was talking about why he chose to dress this way, Samuel was able to both listen and, using his thought speed advantage, develop a way to deal with the problem. He even came up with something that the employee agreed to on the spot.

GREATER AWARENESS

While you have been using the extra time from your Thought Speed Gap all along, you can now commit to a greater awareness and use of the time. Think of using your thought speed as a bonus tool that will help you connect and succeed with your employees.

USE YOUR THOUGHT SPEED GAP

As a Connect & Succeed manager, the Thought Speed Gap is

best used to give you the time to use your Energetic Listening and Targeted Speaking. Here are some examples:

- You search your own memories for personal examples that support what the employee is saying, while you continue to energetically listen. You use your targeted speaking to share the examples. You do not drift off so that you are only thinking about those memories and losing track of the conversation. Instead, you integrate those memories into the conversation.

- While your employee is talking, you develop questions in your mind and then use them in your Targeted Speaking to further explore what she is saying.

- While the person is speaking, you mentally summarize what he is saying. By choosing the points that you think are most important, you then use your targeted speaking to share these points with the employee.

THOUGHT SPEED GAP DISRUPTERS

A note about specifically letting negative or disruptive emotions sidetrack your thinking: The disruption will steal your attention and your thought speed advantage will be used up. If you are only thinking about how angry or upset you are, you will find it more difficult to make full use of the extra time that the Thought Speed Gap gives you. In the end, you are likely to end up feeling more angry or upset.

For example: One of people who reported to me was talking about the problems with a particular project. She said she did not like the direction of the project and believed that my leadership on the project was lacking. Suddenly, I was only thinking about what felt like a personal attack on me, and I could have easily veered away from the Connect & Succeed goal of connecting. The solution in this case was for me to "hold that thought." As I continued to talk with this employee, it became obvious that she was talking about just one specific incident and we were able to easily clear up the misunderstanding around it. I was proud that instead of using my Thought Speed Gap to process my upset, I used it more constructively, and eventually strengthened my connection with this employee.

EXERCISE 32: THOUGHT SPEED GAP

- Before a conversation, remind yourself that you have this extra asset in your back pocket.

- During the conversation, be mindful of how you use the time from the Thought Speed Gap. Is it a fruitful use of the time? Are you using your Thought Speed Gap to your advantage – that is to improve the possibility of connection?

- After the conversation, reflect on your use of the time from the Thought Speed Gap. How could you use it more productively in your next conversation?

USE FULLY FORMED PERSPECTIVES

We all like to think of ourselves as perceptive people. By adopting a Connect & Succeed managerial style, you will elevate your perceptions to Fully Formed Perspectives. This will increase your ability to connect. This will also raise the level of your connection, and your success. This is definitely Advanced Connect & Succeed.

You see, by using just the raw material of our perceptions, we run the risk of making a "read" of a person that is inaccurate. Inaccurate in this case means that you do not understand the other person the way they want to be understood.

It is also important to note here that in the reading of the perceptions, a common default is to translate perceptions into another form – judgments. So if the original perceptions are, in their "rawness," unreliable, then the judgments formed from them are risky. Furthermore, these judgments in general could be the kind of judgments that limit and restrict us, thereby making connection with others more problematic.

But what if you could take the perceptions themselves and generate more in-depth and thoughtful perspectives? These Fully Formed Perspectives would give you greater insight and depth about your employee, and make connection easier and more powerful. You can see then, how mere perceptions have little value to offer when compared to Fully Formed Perspectives.

Let's look at how to make this transformation:

THIN SLICE PERCEPTIONS

Generally, a perception is formed through the senses. There are five senses, but it is most likely that what you see and hear will have the most impact on you. Overall, a perception is a state of awareness about someone, something, or a situation.

To move from your original perceptions to Fully Formed Perspectives, you will begin with the perceptions you have collected through your Energetic Listening and Targeted Speaking. The range of these perceptions can be wide: You might have picked up on what your employee was wearing, how he looked physically or emotionally, what he said, what he did, and all kinds of other things about him and the situation. These will be deeper perceptions because you are using your Connect & Succeed approach, but they are still likely to be Thin Slice Perceptions – perceptions based on a thin slice of information.

It is possible for Thin Slice Perceptions to be accurate. You can get "lucky" in that way. But more frequently, relying on only Thin Slice Perceptions can cause heaps of trouble.

Part of the trouble is our human nature tendency to lock in our initial perceptions. It is human nature to collect a bit of data, make the kind of judgment that does not budge, and move forward with that limitation. The fact is that these initial impressions are then likely to stick until a large amount of new evidence comes in. It is unclear when initial perceptions become "permanent," but it is definitely disconcerting that it can happen so quickly.

For example: One of my coaching clients, Tom, hired some-one to join his team. Tom developed a perception of that person in the interview process and then during the first few weeks on the job, cemented it into a judgment. This person wasn't really working out, but because Tom had cemented in such a positive judgment of this person, he largely ignored the initial negative feedback from other employees. The initial perception of the person "stuck" with him and it was difficult to change until overwhelming evidence forced his hand. Eventually, he had to let go of the positive judgment – and the new employee – and create a fully formed perspective. Unfortunately, he wasted a lot of time before he came to that inevitable conclusion.

As a manager you easily make Thin Slice Perceptions about your employees. For example, you may overhear something about your department's project in the hall or in the cafeteria. While hearing only snippets of information, you could still take that little bit of information and draw broad conclusions. "The project is not going well" may be the thin slice perception that sticks in your mind. If you move ahead with that perception and create judgments out of it, and then find out another project was being talked about, you will not only have wasted time, but could have stirred up trouble.

THIN SLICE PERCEPTION TRIPWIRES

There are also specific tripwires that can affect your Thin Slice Perceptions, including your expectations and need for closure:

EXPECTATIONS

You quite naturally have expectations of each of your employees. Your expectations are often based on the employee's past behavior. These expectations may, or may not, be grounded in current fact or reality. These expectations could be out-dated or simply wrong, but they could still have a big impact on the perceptions you collect from the conversation.

A NEED FOR CLOSURE

Closure is your drive to make sense of people and situations. You speculate, estimate, and in general make guesses about people even if you have very little information to work with. As humans, we naturally do not like things to be "up in the air," so we often take a small amount of information about an employee, and fill it in to satisfy our need for closure. This allows us to create a perception, but you can imagine how off that perception could then be.

This need for closure can take you further away from the goals of Connect and Succeed. You are not doing what you can to accurately focus on and care about the employee. You are not seeking to hear, respect, and value this employee. You are not making the potential for deep connection more likely, especially if an arbitrary perception that emerged out of your need for closure is used.

Example: I was working for a large healthcare company. Specifically, I was working on team building issues with a Senior Vice President in Procurement. I made the assumption that she was similar to other upper management people I had worked with there-a command and control leader. I proceeded on that assumption and in my need for closure "filled in" lots of information about her. I was wrong. She was a very people-oriented leader who very much cared about her employees. Out of my need for closure, I created a thin slice perception that was inaccurate. Once I recognized how thin my slice of perception was, I was able to shift to a fully formed perspective, and our connection flourished.

Note: Sometimes the need for closure can be a tripwire in the opposite direction: When you have too much information, you could, in looking for order and clarity, unconsciously dismiss the information that does not fit tidily into your perception. This then skews the perception.

EXERCISE 33: THIN SLICE PERCEPTIONS

Identify Thin Slice Perceptions from your past:

- Include situations where the Thin Slice Perceptions were not accurate and caused some kind of disruption.

- Include situations where the Thin Slice Perceptions were accurate.

- During a conversation with an employee, recognize that the perceptions you are gathering as a natural part of any interaction are just the first step of understanding this person and how you can best connect with him.

TRANSFORM THE THIN SLICE PERCEPTION INTO A FULLY FORMED PERSPECTIVE

Instead of using one thin slice, you can use the "whole pie." This means that instead of settling for the Thin Slice Perception, you gather more information and create a Fully Formed Perspective. A perspective is based on a more informed foundation because it combines the raw data of your perceptions (even thin slices of it), other information, and reflection.

A Fully Formed Perspective is more useful for connection because it can stand on its own and you will be less tempted to turn it into a judgment. In fact, its very flexibility relies on staying open to new information and a willingness to shift. When you work with Fully Formed Perspectives in understanding your employees, you will be able to make your Energetic Listening and Targeted Speaking an on-going and dynamic process, which is what Connect & Succeed is all about.

EXERCISE 34:
CREATE A FULLY FORMED PERSPECTIVE

Before the Conversation

- Gather some perceptions you have discovered about the employee you will be interacting with. These might come from past conversations, or even the brief interaction you had in setting up the conversation.

- Reflect upon the perceptions, and any other information you have about this employee. Out of this reflection, you will quite naturally create as full a perspective as possible, while remembering that one of the characteristics of a fully formed perspective is that it is flexible and subject to change.

During the Conversation

- You will be gathering perceptions as part of your Connect & Succeed conversation.

- Be careful not to let these perceptions form into judgments.

- Bringing your perceptions through to Fully Formed Perspectives is possible during a conversation, especially the more practiced you are at processing all the "data" collected. Also, if this is an employee you already have a relationship with, you have some Fully Formed Perspectives from your past conversations.

After the Conversation

- Reflect upon all the perceptions gathered, past perspectives formed (including any formed during the last conversation), and any other information, and create a current fully formed perspective. Use this perspective to help you better connect with your employee.

CHAPTER EIGHT

Your Connect & Succeed Strategy

A Connect & Succeed communication style will power you up as a manager. Your success will rise very quickly as you put your Connect & Succeed style into place. The people you report to are going to pick up on your increasing success with your projects and employees. They will also begin to see you as a great role model and leader in terms of both communication and success. This all means that you will need to step up as a leader as well as a connection-level communicator.

Yes, bringing a Connect & Succeed style into your work as a manager is a big deal. This also means that it will take some time and effort as well as a willingness to step up. Therefore, to take your career to the next level, you want to have a Connect & Succeed strategy.

Having a strategy will motivate and guide you. It will chart your goals and your successes. It will provide you with your own personalized "operating manual."

CREATE YOUR CONNECT & SUCCEED LAUNCH STRATEGY

There are four parts to setting your Connect & Succeed launch strategy in place. Attention to these items will ensure your personal success in adopting a Connect & Succeed communication style:

- Your personal readiness to make the changes necessary for the full adoption of the Connect & Succeed style.

- A plan to deal with employee buy-in to the changes.

- Preparation for truly stepping up to a leadership role—because as a Connect & Succeed manager, you will become a leader.

- A solid sense of your Connect & Succeed goals and a timeline for guidance and accountability.

YOUR READINESS TO MAKE THE TRANSITION

An awareness of how you respond to change is an important factor to look at in implementing a Connect & Succeed style.

When you develop such an awareness, you are better able to prepare and adapt as you move forward.

Individual change is difficult for everyone. Change can be uncomfortable and make you feel like things are "up in the air." Most people like it better when things are "settled." In terms of communication styles, most people have unconsciously settled into a style and are reluctant to change that style.

Honestly, it is probably the benefits of adopting a Connect & Succeed style that make it so attractive to you. This makes it worth dealing with the change factor.

Here are two guidelines that will help with your Connect & Succeed transition:

- First, be patient with yourself. You will be learning your Connect & Succeed skills on the fly, as you interact with your employees, and changing old habits will take time. Take it one step at a time.

- Second, motivate yourself toward change by noting and celebrating your progress. Note that this is not the opposite of being patient. In fact, acknowledging the small successes along the way will help on the patience front.

AN EMPLOYEE BUY-IN PLAN

Your employees will notice that things are changing, and while this will benefit all of your employees, it is possible that some will be a bit thrown by the mere issue of change. After all, they think they have you "figured out." They have each come up with a way to communicate with you... or at least with the "old you." Now you are interacting with them in new ways. Now you are focusing on and caring about them. Now your conversations with them have a different tone. Your employees could feel everything from off-kilter to messed-with.

One of my coaching clients had an employee request a meeting soon after he began to implement his Connect & Succeed style. The employee was worried that my client was about to lay off everyone in the department and was only being "nice" to soften the blow.

In another situation, my client started to schedule more one-on-one meetings as a way to connect. Everyone in the department initially complained that they did not have the time for one-on-one meetings. My client stuck with her decision to have more one-on-one meetings, and eventually, the complaints subsided and the meetings were very successful!

You cannot blame your employees for feeling like a fish out of water. You are asking them to buy-in to your new style, and they will be worried about the change. Their worry about change is part of your preparation because you are the one who will have to either plan for a successful transition for them, or deal with the problems that arise from a rough transition.

Make employee buy-in a natural part of your new Connect & Succeed strategy. Here are a few buy-in tips you can use:

- Let your employees know what is happening. This could range from an announcement to your department about your Connect & Succeed initiative, to more informal "hints" during your discussions with them.

- Encourage employees to share their questions and concerns with you, and answer the questions and concerns with honesty and clarity.

- Share the benefits of the Connect & Succeed communication style with your employees. Be sure to let them know that they will benefit both directly and indirectly.

- Be strong in your determination to make your Connect & Succeed changes, no matter what the level of support from your employees. Do not let initial employee concerns create doubt for you.

YOUR PREPARATION TO LEAD

Prepare to be a leader – because Connect & Succeed managers are leaders!

On one hand, you will lead your employees. Connect & Succeed is all about being conscious in your connections. This consciousness makes all the difference in how your employees perceive you. You have already noticed how you take the responsibility for connection in your Connect & Succeed conversations. By consciously taking this initiative in each conversation, you are setting yourself up to build your platform as a leader. This will, by the way, feel great!

You might also find yourself standing out among the managers in your company. You are more likely to find managers who are still using a directive style of management and communication, so your style, and its results, will bring the spotlight. Your Connect & Succeed style will become a model for the other managers in your company.

Finally, the people you report to will have to take notice, as the Connect & Succeed benefits show up. You will become a leader for change within your company.

EXERCISE 35:
ARE YOU READY TO CONNECT & SUCCEED?

Readiness to Make the Transition:

- Ask yourself: What personal obstacles, including your attitudes and beliefs, make it more difficult for you to deal with change?

- In what ways is your current communication style working?

- What motivating factors are behind your desire to change to a Connect & Succeed communication style?

- What actions can you take to assure your success as a Connect & Succeed manager?

Employee Buy-in:

- Create a plan for getting your employees to buy in to the change to a Connect & Succeed communication style. Your plan should cover the following:

    - How to announce and present the change
        - Include the benefits of the change.

- Include a complete accounting of what will be asked of the employees in order to make this transition. (For instance, more one-on-one conversations with you.)
- A structure to handle employee questions and concerns.

Prepare to Lead:
- Accept that your role as a Connect & Succeed manager will make you a leader.
- Prepare to be a leader:
  - Visualize yourself as a leader.
  - Reflect on the type of leader you want to be.
  - Look for role models. Read about and research the stories behind your role models.

GOALS AND TIMELINE

You know the many benefits that a Connect & Succeed communication style will bring in general, but in your strategy you want to reflect on what specific benefits you desire for yourself, your employees, your department, and your company. These will be your goals. You will then want to prioritize these goals.

Additionally, a timeline for implementation is important. The timeline provides a "framework" for your Connect & Succeed strategy, and the deadlines are great motivators.

147

EXERCISE 36: GOALS AND TIMELINE

Goals

- Review the benefits of the Connect & Succeed communication style presented in Chapter 1. Using the Connect & Succeed Benefits section as a guideline, list 3-4 goals you would like to achieve.

- With each of your listed goals, write down the specifics of your goals. For instance, if you feel like your department is ineffective in employee problem solving, note the current situation and come up with as specific a goal as possible. This might, for instance, mean a reduction in formal staff complaints, measured per month.

- Add any other goals that you feel are viable and relevant.

- Prioritize your list of goals.

Timeline

- Create a timeline by drawing a horizontal line across a sheet of paper.

- On the left end of the line write today's date.

- On the right end of the line, write a date in the future. Suggestion: 8-12 months out.

- Starting with your top priority goal, write in the goals along the line.

- Give each goal a "due date." Be realistic but committed.

- Put these due dates in your calendar.

CREATE AN OPERATING MANUAL

Creating an operating manual for your Connect & Succeed strategy, will take you deeper into your success. The manual will provide inspiration and accountability.

The elements of your operating manual are:

YOUR CONNECT AND SUCCEED LAUNCH STRATEGY

Your launch strategy is contained in the documents from Exercises 35 and 36, plus any additional notes, reflections, and/or assessments.

THE CONNECT & SUCCEED EXERCISES

The exercises in this book are valuable! Keeping them together and accessible is a wise thing to do. This is the "study guide" part of your operating manual.

Include all documents generated by the exercises in Chapters 2-7. Also include any notes, reflections, and/or assessments that are related to the topics of the exercises.

STANDARD PROCEDURES

With any or all of the exercises, you can create a standard procedure for yourself.

For instance, three to five weeks into implementing the distraction prevention exercise, create standard procedures for dealing with distractions. For conversations in your office you might create a standard checklist of things to do before the meeting: Mute your phone, let your assistant know you will be unavailable for a specific amount of time, and stand up to stretch for two minutes.

TRACKING NOTES

There are two items you might want to track: Your successes and your connections. You can track your successes either chronologically or by Connect and Succeed topic (For example: Energetic Listening: Pinpointing Nonverbal Signals.) In tracking your connections, it is a good idea to do this by employee.

In keeping track, you will want to include any notes, reflections, and/or assessments that are relevant.

CONNECT & SUCCEED TRAINING

Connect & Succeed training options are available and include personal and group coaching for you or your managers and/or employees. There are also seminars, including an introduction to Energetic Listening and an introduction to Connect & Succeed, as well as more extensive training programs that are custom designed for your company, and combine seminars, presentations, and/or coaching and consulting.

For more information, contact Dave Bennett:

info@connectandsucceed.com

www.connectandsucceed.com

COMMON GROUND
CONNECTION
SUMMARY

CONNECT THROUGH COMMON GROUND

- Frame Your Connect & Succeed Mindset

- Connect Through Common Ground

- Advanced Connection

YOUR CONNECT & SUCCEED STRATEGY

- Your Connect & Succeed Launch Strategy

- Your Operating Manual

- Connect & Succeed Training

AFTERWORD

Connect & Succeed

You are now on our way to success! You have covered lots of ground, but it is ground that will definitely up your connection abilities, and therefore bring on the success.

First and foremost, I congratulate you! The Connect & Succeed communication style will change your life, as a manager and as a person. Furthermore, this positive change will ripple out to your employees, and throughout your company.

Together we can engage and motivate employees at workplaces around the world. Let's connect and let's succeed!

WORKS CITED

Dale Carnegie Training. "How to Engage Employees by Fostering Positive Emotion" Dale Carnegie Training, n.d. Web. 14 Sept. 2015. http://www.dalecarnegie.com/employee-engage ment/how-to-engage-employees-by-fostering-positive-emo tions-infographic.

Patchen, Sally. Personal interview. 17 Apr. 2015.

Summar, Patrick. Personal interview. 28 Sept. 2015.

INDEX

A

Actively acknowledge, 85, 98-99, 115, 117
Attention span
    Expanding, 20, 35, 36-37, 40
    Refocusing, 41
    Train for longer spans, 42
    Meditation, 43

C

Carnegie, Dale, 4, 13, 25
Collaboration and teamwork, 21
Commitment, 6, 9, 12-14, 39
    Employee retention, 14
Common ground
    Definition, 24
    Find common ground, 28
    Seek mutual understanding, 89
    Identify, 89, 93
    Speak of, 89, 94
    Mindset, 123, 126
Common ground connection
    Spark of connection, 27
Connect and succeed
    Definition, 5
    Actions, 7-8
    Benefits, 9
    Conversation, 7-8
    Tools, 24, 27, 99, 110-113
    Keeping track, 31
    Mindset, 104-107
    Launch strategy, 142-147

Connection, advanced
    Thought speed gap, 110-112, 132
    Search your memories, 112
    Mentally summarize, 112
    Thin slice perceptions, 134-136, 138
    Fully formed perspectives, 134-135, 139-140
Cultural differences, 61, 63

D

Disagreements, 24, 27, 97-98, 113-115
Distraction strategies
    Prevent, 32
    Eliminate, 33, 37
    Identify, 33
    Acknowledge, 33
    Be proactive, 37
    Manage, 38
    Prepare, 39

E

Emotional contagion, 32, 49, 51-53, 86-88
Emotions, 13, 44-46, 51-53, 57, 85-88, 103, 132
    Underlying, 49
    Strong sensitivity to, 50
    Tune into, 76
Emotion-based bond, 19

Empathy, 110-113
Employee development, 13
Employee
    Retention, 13
    Rejection, 18
Energetic listening, 7, 8, 20-23,
    29-33
    Contagious, 19, 21
    As a virus, 21
    Pay attention, 35
    For subtle meanings, 36
    Deal with distractions, 37
    Expand your attention span,
    39
    Raise your connect awareness,
    44
Engagement, 9-14, 83, 91, 125

F
Feedback, 12, 90-92, 101, 136
Feeling cared about, 108
Focus and care about employees,
    19, 108

H
Heard, respected and valued, 7,
    25, 97
Homophobic comments, 77, 78
Honesty, 87, 91, 145
Human nature, 124, 135, 137

I
Intentional communication,
    17-18
Introvert, 7, 62

L
Language, 46-48, 51, 56, 78-79,
    85, 108

M
Meeting at the meaning level,
    100
Motivate yourself, 143
Multi-tasking, 35
Mutual respect, 27

N
Nonverbal communication
    Percentage of meaning, 48
    Consider context, 52
    Complexity, 57
    Flexible baselines, 57
    Mimicking, 85
    Closure 137-138
Nonverbal pinpointing, 23, 55,
    56, 59, 65, 68
    Identify and translate signals,
    60
    Cluster and baseline, 52, 55,
    64
Nonverbal signals, 57, 60, 61, 63-
    67, 68, 83-84, 86
Nonverbal stereotyping, 61

O
Obstacles to connection, 106
One-on-one conversations, 9, 74
Open and honest feedback, 96
Operating manual
    Launch strategy, 149

Exercises, 149
Procedures and checklists,
   149-150
Tracking notes, 150

P
Patchen, Sally, 29
Patience, 143
Productivity, 14, 17-18
   Personal, 11
   Company, 18
Praise, 15
Problem solving, 15-16, 115, 148

Q
Questions, 38, 81, 91-92, 99,
   101-103

R
Racist comments, 77-78
Raise your connection awareness
   Self-awareness, 44-45
   Picking up subtle meanings
      44, 46
Remembering what we hear, 22
Risk being open, 21

S
Self-awareness, 45
Sexist comments, 77-78
Shared information, 19
Speaking style
   Speak in short increments, 80
   Use congruent nonverbals,
      80-82

Match nonverbal signals, 85
Success as a manager, 4, 49
Summar, Patrick, 16
Supporting the speaker, 24, 101,
   105

T
Targeted speaking
   Speak with clarity, 26, 74
   Tailor your message, 26, 66,
      75-76
   Consider your speaking style,
      66
   Offer common ground, 66
   Match your vocabulary, 77
   Be willing, 139
Tune in
   Tone and language, 46-47
   Emotions, 50
Turnover, 14

V
Verbal acknowledgments, 99
   Use audio-flow comments,
      99-100
   Paraphrase, 100-101
   Ask relevant questions,
      101-103
   Make supportive comments,
      101-103

W
Weave of conversations, 30
Workplace environment, 17

ABOUT THE AUTHOR

David W. Bennett, Ph.D. is a principal at Common Ground Communication, and creator of the Connect & Succeed Communication Style. He offers communication seminars to companies worldwide, as well as consulting and coaching programs for middle management. Additionally, he teaches university courses, both on campus and online.

For more information on seminars, consulting, and coaching, contact Dave at: 949-235-8571 or info@connectandsucceed.com